Unleashing the Tigress Within

How to Attract Great Men into Your Life

By Gregg Michaelsen

Copyright © 2020 Gregg Michaelsen and Confidence Builder LLC.

All rights reserved. No part of this publication may be reproduced, stored in a retrieval system, or transmitted in any form or by any means, electronic, mechanical, photocopying, recording, or otherwise, without written permission of the publisher.

DISCLAIMER: As a male dating coach I am very good at what I do because of my years of studying the nuances of interpersonal relationships. I have helped thousands of women understand men. That said, I am not a psychologist, doctor or licensed professional. So do not use my advice as a substitute if you need professional help.

Women tell me how much I have helped them, and I truly hope that I can HELP you too in your pursuit of that extraordinary man! I will provide you with powerful tools. YOU need to bring me your willingness to listen and CHANGE!

Contents

1. Welcome to the First Day of the New You! 1
Because now, You have Me!. 2
This Time, it Will be Different! 3
Start Your Training Today 4

2. The Four-Minute Mile and the Power of Belief . 5

3. The First Five Steps Required for Dating Success 7
STEP 1: It's Time to Unveil Your Uniqueness 8
STEP 2: Acknowledge Your Own Value. 10
STEP 3: See One. Do One. Teach One. 12
STEP 4: Set Boundaries. 14
STEP 5: Shoot for Above Average! 16
This is About Desire to Be Better 17

4. Crafting Your Vision 19
Get Clear and Detailed 19
Let Your Vision become You. 20
Feel Your Vision 22

5. It's Time to Change Your Thinking 25
Change Your Idea of Where Happiness Comes From. . . 26
Understand Where Security Comes From 27
Become a Confident Woman 28
Becoming the Chooser, instead of the Chosen 30
Slow Your Roll. 31
Debunking the Common Myths of Dating 33
How to stop falling for these myths 42
The Ultimate Key to Dating and Finding the Man of Your Dreams. 43
Now, to get This New Mindset Working for You 44

6. Your Inner Game 47

7. Branding Yourself for Dating 51
Marketing and Dating? They're Practically Synonymous . 51
It's Your Uniqueness that Makes the Biggest Difference . . 52
Define Your Dating Brand 54
Communicating Your Brand 60
And Now...to Target the Right Type of Man 62
Building Your Brand 63
Why All of this Matters to Your Dating Life 68
Now It's Time 69

8. Unlocking the Power of Gratitude 71
Benefits of Gratitude 73
Practicing Gratitude Daily 75

9. Making the Right First Impression 79
Men are Visual 80
What is Attractive? 81
What Else do Men "Look" At? 83

10. How to Know Which Guys are the Good Guys 85
The User 86
The Loser 99
Four Test Dates to Weed Out Users and Losers 108
The Snoozers 111
Mr. Right 116

11. Meeting Men Where They Are 117
Owning the Bar Scene 119
Unleashing Your Inner Tigress at a High-End Event . . 124
Sporting Events 125

12. Unleashing Your Inner Tigress 127
Your Inner Tigress is Sexy 128
Your Inner Tigress Takes Risks 136

Meet and Attract Him *137*
Encourage Him to Approach *140*
Be Prepared with an Adjusted Mindset *140*
You Have the Tools Now *144*

13. It's Time to Meet Men on Your Terms. . . . 145
Attend a Local Single's Event *145*
Go to a Sports Bar *146*
Get in Line *146*
Love Your Single Status *147*

14. Examining Why You've Dated the Wrong Type of Guy in the Past. 149
Lack of Confidence *149*
Not Knowing What You Really Want *149*
Likes attract Likes. *150*
You Went for the Hot Guy Instead of the Right Guy . . . *151*
You Didn't Take the Time to Truly Get to Know One Another *151*
You Share Similar Baggage *152*
You Don't Understand Where Happiness Comes From . . *153*
You Were Tired of Being the Single One *153*
You Initiated a Relationship on Faulty Reasoning . . . *153*
You Ignored Many Red Flags *154*
You Thought You Could Fix Him *155*

15. The Best First Date 157
Heighten the Emotion *157*
We're Really the Same *159*
When Dining Out *161*
Let Him Be A Guy *161*
What to Wear *162*

A Bit About Your Drill Sergeant 165

Get the Word Out to Your Friends 169

Welcome to the First Day of the New You!

Entering, or re-entering the dating scene *and* finding a great guy is no small task. You've probably been looking for your great guy for a while now and I'm guessing you are a little frustrated.

Where *are* all the great men and *how on earth* do you attract one, once you find him? You may believe all the great men are taken. Your best friend found the last one and they're engaged, so there goes that.

Your problem isn't that there aren't any great men. Your problem is that you seem to keep meeting and dating the same guy. Oh, he might be a little different here and there—different hair, different eyes, but in general, he's the same guy.

He treats you the same way other guys have treated you in the past. He acts the same way around his friends as the other guys you've dated. You may reach a similar point of frustration in each relationship before they seem to crumble apart, leaving you devastated and frustrated.

So why will this time be different?

Because now, You have Me!
That's right. You have me, Gregg, as your sidekick.

I'm going to be the one with a gentle hand on your back, guiding you and encouraging you to try things differently this time. You're going to acquire new tools to attract and keep the man of your dreams. And you'll do all this while I protect you from the losers and users.

Thousands of women of all ages have benefitted from this advice, both through my books and in person. I'm a take action kind of guy, so on many Saturday nights, I go out and find a group of women, just like you and your friends, and I hang out with them.

I text their boyfriends for them and they learn how to manage the men in the room by deciphering what type of guys they are, then they get the confidence boost they need to go after the guys they like.

If you're thinking this isn't you - that the bar scene isn't your thing, know that I also go to piano bars, attend wine tastings and do video summits with the best in the world.

Regardless of your age—I have you covered.

They've learned it and so can you!

This Time, it Will be Different!
This book is designed to get you moving and shaking. I have exercises to go along with each chapter and you can find them in the free gift below!

**GET YOUR FREE WORKBOOK:
www.whoholdsthecardsnow.com/
unleashing-the-tigress-within-workbook-signup**

This book is about helping you be happier in every part of your life. Happy people are positive people and positive women attract great men! Learn how to put your happiness on full display for the men you meet.

Unleashing the Tigress Within is about action. Yes, you can read this book and you will get a lot out of it, but in order to change yourself and your dating outcomes, action is required. If you only want to read without taking any action to make those changes, you may as well stop now and find a different book.

If I didn't feel the exercises in the workbook were worth your time and energy, they wouldn't be here, but the truth is that many women have benefitted from completing these exercises and they will work for you!

And, before you decide you're too old, what's inside this book is for women of *all* ages! You're never too old!

This is no joke! What you're about to learn will bring you higher confidence, an improved social life and more quality men. When you have a larger pool of great men to choose from, your odds of success increase exponentially.

If you're not a woman who wants to explore, date and eventually find a guy to settle down with, this book isn't for you. You're not going to learn how to be a hook-up artist. You're going to learn how to snag Mr. Right.

Start Your Training Today

While, in theory, you could fly through the chapters in a couple of hours, it's not wise. Each chapter and exercise builds on those you've completed before, so take your time and do the work.

Instant gratification is nice but waiting for long-term gratification is better. Do the work now to enjoy the fruits of your labor later—I promise you, it's worth it!

The Four-Minute Mile and the Power of Belief

Roger Bannister wasn't *supposed* to run the mile in under four minutes. That's what everyone told him, from teammates to fans to running coaches and the rest of society. For thousands of years, breaking this record was simply deemed to be impossible.

Nobody believed that the human body could run a mile in less than four minutes. This was the pure, unquestioned truth. Until 1954, when Roger Bannister decided to envision the impossible and believe in what others simply couldn't.

On a rainy, windy day, in less than ideal conditions, Roger Bannister ran a 3:59—an achievement heard round the world. In doing so, he broke a world record, made history and completely transformed the status quo of what people believed was achievable.

After Bannister was able to achieve the sub-four mile, it only took 46 days for someone to break his record. Think about that for a minute. For thousands of years, the world placed a limit on what was possible - until there was someone bold and powerful enough to break through it, opening the door for countless others.

The lesson here is that your own personal beliefs will transcend what others think is possible for you. Roger Bannister had a vision other people thought was crazy. He put his vision to work and ultimately changed the face of sport and human spirit forever.

It's entirely within your power and experience to harness the same tool Roger Bannister did on that amazing day in 1954. It's within you, ready and willing to be heard and shared with the world.

Now, a word of caution: belief can also work to constrict instead of expanding you. Negative thinking and a mentality of scarcity can have the opposite effect.

If we look at the great achievers in all aspects of life throughout history and those who created and transformed industries, you'll notice they simply never listened to the naysayers, the critics and those who thought they were crazy.

The First Five Steps Required for Dating Success

I'm all about getting down to business, but first, it's important to walk through this five-step process to build the kind of confidence quality men are seeking. Taking these first five steps will get you headed in the right direction.

Review the information contained in these five steps multiple times. You will benefit most by reading and rereading these steps a few times. Become familiar with them. Do the exercises in the workbook and feel yourself growing more confident!

Pay attention to the next rom com you watch. At some point, I can guarantee you that the guy will say he's attracted to the confidence of the girl. Men love confident women. They're drawn to confident women like a moth to the flame.

Finding a great guy is your prize for doing the hard work you'll be doing in the upcoming chapters. You may read some of the exercises and shake your head, believing you can't do it, but I implore you to at least *try* to do them. Put forth your best effort. Be Roger Bannister—well, a female Roger Bannister anyway.

If you're not willing to change yourself, you're going to continue drawing in those losers and users you've dated in the past. Think about it this way—the common denominator in your past relationships isn't the men, it's you, so for your dating success to change, *you* need to change.

Each of these steps builds on the one before. When you combine these steps, you become a force to be reckoned with!

STEP 1: It's Time to Unveil Your Uniqueness

When I go out on Saturday nights, I see quite a few women I like to call female robots. They've taken their cues from magazines and television. They believe that the best way to catch a guy is by flashing as much skin as possible.

Nothing could be further from the truth.

The woman who intrigues *me* is the woman who is dressed nice. She is comfortable in herself and her clothing. Her choice in clothing shows her care for, and confidence in her body. And, at the same time, it isn't too revealing; it leaves a lot to my imagination.

The woman who draws in great men also isn't concerned about carrying high-end purses, wearing high-end shoes and pounds of makeup. Her attractiveness comes from her belief that she is worthy of a great man. It comes from having a life outside of dating that's full of hobbies and friends—hobbies and friends she isn't willing to give up for *any* man.

Her confidence resonates through her body language. Her facial movements alone can attract a guy without him even knowing why. Tap into this!

Don't be that female robot. Be yourself. If you want to show up to a bar in a tie-dye floor length skirt with a tank top and flat sandals, go for it. If it's the real you, do it. Don't try to be someone you aren't. Wear jeans and a nice top or a pencil skirt and spike heels, if that's what you're *comfortable* in.

A great man will be intrigued by your confidence, not your clothing. He will be attracted to the confident walk you possess and the way in which you look right at him, then look away.

Being you means being unique. It means dressing the way you want to dress, drinking what you want to drink, watching the football game if it interests you or dancing to the music if that seems like a fun idea. Know what you like, how you're comfortable and where you like to be and then do it, wear it and be it.

What happens when you start allowing your uniqueness to shine through? People are drawn to you. People want to get to know you. They want to hang out with you and learn more about you. Men included! Great men especially!

Along with figuring out what you like to wear, be and do, take some time to figure out what your dream is and then plan to start living that dream (don't worry, I'll help you in a few minutes!) Make this a priority in your life and watch men begin to take notice!

Your first exercise will help you begin to uncover your own uniqueness. If you don't have the workbook yet, you can **download it at www.whoholdsthecardsnow.com/unleashing-the-tigress-within-workbook-signup.**

STEP 2: Acknowledge Your Own Value

Once you begin following your dreams, being, doing and wearing what you like, instead of what Vogue told you to, you will notice that you become a little busier. Your time is filling up, which makes it more valuable and precious.

"But Gregg, if I'm doing all of this, how will I have time to meet great men?"

You'll meet a great guy along the way. You'll meet him *while* you are pursuing your dreams. This is the best way to meet a great guy. Much more effective than online dating because you're meeting men who are doing the things you like to do. You'll want to brainstorm and prioritize the activities you love *that include men*. As much as you may like yoga, keep this as a secondary option for now.

Men will find your busy lifestyle interesting and even mysterious. Great men are attracted to women who aren't always available because it shows them you have a life outside of trying to reel them in.

No great man wants to become your top priority, regardless of what he says. He does not want you doting over him 24/7 and he does not want to be your new hobby, in lieu of the Yoga and art classes you were taking before you met.

He will be interested in your involvement in these activities. He will find getting a date with you to be challenging and he will work hard to make sure he is worthy of time on your calendar!

Another great thing happens when you reprioritize your life and fill it with pursuing your goals and dreams. The losers and users you once found attractive are now unappealing. You begin to see them for who they truly are! This is a great feeling! You no longer want to give up your time pursuing a priority to chase after another loser.

And those losers are out there in force, but now you're worthy of great men. You can seek them out unlike before when you had no confidence or understanding of how men think.

Exercise 2 is waiting for you in your workbook.

STEP 3: See One. Do One. Teach One.

There are many instances when you can gain status and influence by helping others with a skill you possess. That might come in the form of being a mentor for someone, or maybe you'll have an opportunity to teach a class.

If you're a businesswoman, you might be able to run a workshop at a local business incubator for people just starting out, to teach them what you've learned.

Whatever it is, giving back or helping others, it is a great way to not only build your confidence but increase your status and influence in your community.

Why is this important? Increasing your status increases your intrigue—it ups the mystery and challenge factor. At the same time, it weeds out the losers who don't dare mess with a confident woman like you!

While doing this, you meet more people who share your goals, dreams, and skills. Whether you're teaching a group of business owners how to design a website or you're playing Bridge with the senior citizens at the local nursing home, you're expanding your circle a little wider and casting a bigger net.

While you're adding people, who are more like you, into your life, it's important to weed out the people who *aren't supportive* of the new you.

These are also people who don't support your dreams and may even throw roadblocks up to keep you from realizing your dreams. They do this because they sense they are being left behind—they're being replaced, and they don't like that idea.

While you're narrowing the field of negativity, remain kind. Just try to reduce your contact with these people. Respond slower to their texts. Hang out with them less often. Start to slowly decrease the time you spend with them.

One of two things will happen. They will either realize you've got something good going on and ask how they too can make changes, or they will gravitate to one another and close the circle without you inside. Either way is fine.

Ironically, the type of guy you don't want to date anymore, will do the same. Funny how this dominoes!

Men are attracted to powerful, influential women. They are attracted to rock stars and movie stars because they feel they are more important than the average followers in life, but you don't need to be a rock star or a movie star to become his status symbol. You just need to be you—confident, interesting you.

Exercise 3 is waiting...

STEP 4: Set Boundaries

Boundaries are difficult, especially if you've never set them before. Boundaries are the things which enable you to maintain your uniqueness, hang onto your values and pursue your goals.

As you reprioritize your life, you may find that hanging out twice a week at the local bar isn't your thing any longer. You may find that you'd rather spend one of those evenings at a photography class, learning to cook or participating in local community theater. The possibilities are endless.

Still, your friends may try to drag you along to your old hangouts. You must decide how often you want to participate. Maybe it's every other week, maybe it's once a week instead of twice. Maybe it's not at all.

Whatever you decide determines the boundary you need to establish.

Your friends will try to convince you to go with them, instead of doing what you want to do. Your boundary becomes the frequency by which you will hang out with them. The harder you try to hold onto a boundary, the more determined your friends will become in trying to coerce you into breaking that boundary.

Those who have run some part of your life in the past won't like giving up that control, even if it's to you.

It's also important to establish boundaries with men. How do you expect to be treated? Are you willing to wait a week for a guy to respond to a text? *(Hint: waiting a day or two is not out of the possibility so don't set that boundary too tight!)*

At what point will you know your relationship has reached a level at which you would consider having sex with a man? When would you move in? Get engaged? Get married? What qualities do you expect a man to show you before you consider something long-term?

Think about these things now, while your common sense is in control, instead of later when you could be blinded by your heart.

Think about the areas of your life in which you've felt like a doormat in the past. During what activities, with which people, have you felt the most like you wanted to be anywhere else doing anything else? When do you feel as if people are completely ignoring your choices or preferences?

Those are the places in which boundaries need to be inserted. There is never a time during which you should feel used or your wishes should be ignored.

Know what you will tolerate out of people and then stand up for yourself! Set and maintain those boundaries. High confidence, high self-esteem people will respect your boundaries. Users and losers (male and female) will ignore, push or abuse your boundaries. Every. Single. Time.

Complete Exercise 4 now to set your boundaries

STEP 5: Shoot for Above Average!

Yes, average is okay, but above average is better, don't you agree?

I don't have a problem with average, but why should you settle? Why not aspire to be above average in at least some areas of your life? Can you work a little harder at your job to excel at something? Can you take a class in something to get better?

Personally, I am always trying to learn. I'm always seeking new ways of doing things, meeting new people, aspiring to be better in all aspects of my life. I even try to work smarter!

This isn't just about you, either. This is also about how you treat other people. It's about giving more time to the people who respect your boundaries and support your dreams. It's about giving less time to people who constantly push your boundaries and try to keep you down.

I can't think of a time in my life where I didn't want to be a better person, at least in one area of my life. When I was a young adult, I wanted to learn construction. Now, I own my own construction company.

Later in my adulthood, I wanted to understand why so many relationships end in failure, including my own, so I began talking to people, studying couples and learning what successful couples have that unsuccessful ones don't. I still want to learn about people, which is why I go out all the time and hang out with people I don't know.

But I also want to learn new things, like new techniques in construction or new ways to improve my writing for you. I seek out new tools to deliver information to you in a way that works for you.

Always learning. Always growing. Always seeking to be above average. Let's get you to do the same.

This drive to be above average is yet another quality that will make you appealing to men. It makes you mysterious and interesting. It makes you someone they want to spend time with so they can peel back the layers and say, "Wow, I thought I knew her!"

These things will come as you identify and go after your goals and dreams. Much of what you've learned about the previous four steps will make this last step an easy one, mindless even.

This is About Desire to Be Better

Without a desire to change, you're wasting your time reading the remainder of this book. If you've read these five steps and you're not sure you want to make these changes, it's time to close this book and go hang out with your same friends. Keep dating the same men. Keep entering relationships that won't succeed. You've been there and done that.

Okay, wait, you're still reading. So, you do want to change!?! That is the best news I've heard all day, and it's the best decision you've made today!

If I've done my job so far, you're now excited at the possibilities. You've already dug into the activities I've included so far, and you are already feeling a little different. Maybe you can't pinpoint why you feel different, but you know you do.

That's great news for you. It means you're well on your way to dating success!

Crafting Your Vision

Get Clear and Detailed

If you pull the average person off the street and ask them what they truly want out of life, they'll likely say, "I want to be happy" or some variation on those words which are rooted in the social ideals passed down to us by others.

Maybe they'll go a step further and start defining happy, "I want to be married, make great money and have a family". The problem with these answers is that there's no true, riveting detail applied to them, they are as generic as it gets.

Additionally, there is no deep-rooted, concrete *why* that stands out. Many times, these are things others have told them they should want, but nobody takes the time to define what happy looks like. There's a universal law which states if you don't paint your vision as detailed and specific as possible, other people are going to paint it for you.

That means one day, you may wake up in the middle of a life you didn't design, but rather, was designed for you by other's wishes, be it your parents, family, schoolteachers, authorities or others.

Do you truly want that? I doubt the answer is yes but ask yourself that question and see what feelings and thoughts come up.

The opposite of having others define your life for you is living with intention—crafting a detailed vision of where you truly want to go. This is hard for many people because issues of self-worth beliefs, what they think they deserve, or fear of what others may think.

We tend to dim our own brightness and not dream too big in fear of pushing others away or being labeled crazy, arrogant, weird or any other name you can imagine.

Surrender to your greatness, let go of the fear and harness your inner dreamer and creator right now. It's your time... believe that.

Let Your Vision become *You*

Once you start getting clear about your vision, you will notice an extra spring in your step. You may, seemingly out of nowhere, have more energy, feel more fulfilled and see the world a little differently, even if you're still in a job you don't love, or you haven't made progress with your goals.

It's the power of being part of the 1% who spend time on this important exercise. You may find the daily frustrations, which once bothered you, simply don't impact you nearly as much as they once did. Maybe you got a couple hours less sleep, but you still wake up with energy.

These are the signs you're moving in the right direction, the direction of living a life of internal inspiration, not external motivation. The difference between the two is that inspiration is something which comes from deep within, while motivation is something which comes from beyond—a source outside of ourselves which may guilt or shame you into acting.

Most people see motivation as a good thing, and it can be at times, but it doesn't last or create nearly as much power as inspiration does. Once you've crafted your vision, you'll tie your personal identity to that vision. Your vision will become part of who you are.

You begin by crafting a plan of action, targets and goals that are directly in line with your vision. The world is full of dreamers and those who still have that childhood curiosity and thinker inside of them, but there are very few dreamers who take action. The way you merge your vision from being something you simply want to making it who you are is simple: **take action!**

Many people get lost in this massive vision—it's so far out of their current perception of reality they simply don't do anything. You've probably been there before. You had a large project to complete and didn't know where to start, so you spent most of the time procrastinating until the deadline was so real, you created a haphazard result.

Your beliefs drive your behaviors, which ultimately drive your results.

Feel Your Vision

It's not enough to write down your vision. One of the keys in starting to change your reality and beliefs around that vision is to go deep into it and feel the vision. This means you use a visualization technique which allows you to *feel* what it's like to accomplish that goal.

For example, if your vision includes having an unbelievable, connected relationship with a significant other, take yourself to that place mentally. Feel what it's like to wake up next to that person every morning. Envision what it's like to operate throughout your day in that state. Explore how it changes the way you walk into a room or interact with a stranger.

Your vision needs to be that detailed and specific or it won't have nearly the powerful result it could have. This is where goal setting and vision become very, very real.

Your mind doesn't know the difference between the reality you're seeing right now and the imagination you use when you visualize. With the method you're about to discover, you'll be able to continue to anchor your mind with this feeling—allowing yourself to believe it's possible. You will be able to go to that place of accomplishment any time you'd like.

You can create your vision with Exercise 5.

It's Time to Change Your Thinking

Wait. Isn't that what the first chapter was all about?

Well, yes, but now, it's time to expand on what you learned. Remember in the beginning, I said those steps were *just* the beginning? Well, hang onto your hat because things are about to get interesting!

I'm excited for you right now. Do you want to know why?

Yes?

Okay, well I'm excited for you because you're single.

Please don't yell at me—hear me out. The changes I want you to make, the changes included in this book, can only happen when you're single.

Why?

Because when your single there's no influence from others breathing down your neck and determining your fate. If you're in a relationship (especially with a loser) while you're reading, your judgment and your desire to participate in the challenges and activities won't be where it should be to see meaningful change.

So, again, I'm excited for you right now.

Change Your Idea of Where Happiness Comes From

The first thing we need to clear up is that you do not need a man in your life to be happy. I want you to write that in big red letters on a piece of paper and stick it to your bathroom mirror:

"I do not need a man in my life to be happy!"

I know you may think you do, but happiness doesn't come from having a man in your life. It comes from living a life that is true to your values, pursuing your dreams and goals, creating your true vision for your life, being surrounded by people who support and love you for who you are, and several other factors.

It's very important for you to understand this or else nothing here will hit home in the way it needs to. Your happiness comes from within you, not from an outside force, like a man.

This internal happiness factor expands into all areas of your life as well. For example, if you don't like your job, why is that? Is it because it doesn't align with your values? Is it because you see no growth potential? Is it because you're being bullied or ignored by your boss?

You can change all those factors by finding a job that aligns with your values or one that offers you the growth you desire. You can get out of the line of fire from bosses who should never have been promoted. You can make the change to be happy in your job.

This mindset expands into all your relationships as well, which you have already learned about. Happiness comes from hanging out with people who support your goals and dreams, people who encourage you and respect your boundaries.

It expands into your life outside of work, your friends and eventually, your ideal relationship. Pursuing your goals should make you happy. It should excite you and get you all fired up.

You can press on and do Exercise 6 now.

Understand Where Security Comes From

Just like happiness, security doesn't come from having a man, any old man, in your life. Feeling secure comes from being smart and a little streetwise. Security comes from being financially smart and emotionally in control.

I know it's scary to walk from the office door to your car in the dark and yes, I'd certainly feel better if there was someone walking alongside you, but I also understand that if you walk confidently with your head high and your focus on what's going on around you, you will look like someone in charge. Wait until you get home to get on your phone!

If you're worried about physical security, take a self-defense class, don't date a bozo. Surely you can see the difference.

Being secure is part self-esteem, part confidence, part common sense and part bravery. I'm not saying that there won't be times when you feel a little shaky, but if you take that self-defense class and boost your self-esteem and confidence, those times will be fewer and farther between.

Become a Confident Woman

Like I said earlier, I'm excited for you, but this time for a different reason. Being single gives you the opportunity to spoil yourself a little. It's a great time for visiting old friends, taking a vacation, inserting some self-care into your weekly routine and growing.

Being single is also an adventure. This journey you are on can easily be expressed as an adventure. You're trying new things, exploring new ways of doing things. You're on a journey to become a new, better version of yourself. It's the journey to become the quintessential you—unique, special, intriguing, happy and secure.

Before you get yourself settled into a new relationship, tick a few items off your bucket list, or create a bucket list if you don't have one yet. Really dig into your goals and nail a few of them.

Every day, I receive questions asking how someone can become more confident. The answer is so much easier than people think it is.

Before you go on, try Exercise 7

The answer is that you start living your own, unique life, designed just for you, by you. You take things that scare the b'jeepers out of you and you face them. Ride that rollercoaster. Sky dive. Do the adventure camp activities like zip-lining and bungee jumping. Stare down a scary spider. Eat dinner out alone.

Do something you've always wanted to do but have been too afraid to try. For some, this might be writing a book. For others, it might be painting a picture or starting your own business. Whatever it is, *go for it!* And this most certainly is meant for you too, my over 50 or over 60 reader!

Never stop pursuing growth and positive change in your life! You would be amazed to know how many of my readers are over 35, 45, 55 and yes, 65! There is always time to be a better version of yourself than you were yesterday.

Becoming the Chooser, instead of the Chosen

I want to ask you to do something and I want you to think long and hard about your answer, okay?

Why, when it is one of the most important decisions you'll make in your life, would you leave the choice of who you'll spend the rest of your life with up to chance?

Why are you allowing men to choose you, instead of choosing men for yourself?

Right now, I imagine your method of meeting men is to dress in something sexy, hang out with your friends, flash a smile at a cute guy across the room and hope he approaches.

Why?

When you recognize that you're the chooser, rather than waiting for a player to choose you, you've reached a great point in the dating process and you will know that your confidence is on the rise!

Wanting to date the cute guy was fine for high school, but now, you're a grown woman who is making what could be a life-long decision and you want to just let it happen?

Perhaps when I phrase it that way, you see how silly it seems.

You are completely in control of which men you date, and it should *not* be the ones who approach with the smooth, polished lines, the chiseled great features and the top-notch wardrobe.

Pay attention to the quiet guy in the corner who is probably perspiring like crazy because he wants to approach you so badly and yet, he hasn't polished his lines by approaching thousands of other women. He isn't comfortable approaching you because he finds you to be very attractive and he doesn't want to mess it up.

Go ahead and flash him a smile and open your body language to let him know it's safe to approach. Instead of huddling with your girlfriends, create a space for him beside you and be patient with him when he does fumble his line—the line he's been practicing ever since you walked into the room!

Slow Your Roll

See if any of this sounds familiar.

You meet a guy and he's drop-dead gorgeous, he's got the smoothest lines, he makes you laugh, and he says all the right things. After the first date, you're trying to decide if you want a June or December wedding and how long you should wait for kids.

Then, at the end of the first date, he kisses you and you're sure this is your forever guy. You've got him locked in. You're ready to trot him off to meet your parents, your friends and your coworkers.

The next date happens, and he drags you off to bed. Wow, you had sex already? This guy must be really serious! You're sure now that a wedding is just a formality.

Here's the thing. First, this guy is probably a user or player, but you missed that because you put blinders on. A lack of confidence let you believe he's the one, without seeing the true man. He's saying and doing all the right things to accomplish just what he did—to sleep with you as soon as possible.

Getting dumped is just a matter of time.

Secondly, if we assume that by some stroke of luck, this guy isn't a player, and instead is actually a great guy (even though no great guy would ask you to have sex on a second date and expect you to say yes), he's really just enjoying the process of getting to know you.

You're ticking off milestones and he's just having fun. Slow your roll. Allow the relationship to unfold naturally, without forcing next steps. There is no hurry. Responding to the noise of a biological clock doesn't do you any good if you end up divorced anyway, so just slow down.

Men's mouths get ahead of their intentions all the time and this can be why they back off and run. A man says he'll take you to Italy, and then he realizes he shouldn't have said that, and he disappears.

Is this okay? Of course not.

That's why it's up to you to slow down and look at his actions to decipher his true intentions - not his words.

When you're struggling to find the right guy, it's easy to glom onto myths about dating, in order to avoid believing that the change required needs to come from within.

Don't get me wrong, I believe you're a fantastic woman who deserves to meet her Mr. Right. I truly do! But, do you believe it?

Right.

Debunking the Common Myths of Dating

MYTH #1: There just aren't enough great men out there.

Okay, this one is easy. You're reading this book, and probably others, to improve something in your life. You're seeking personal growth. All my books are about personal growth and I've sold hundreds of thousands of books, for women *and* for men.

It's easy to think the worst in people, especially in the climate we live in, but the truth is there are millions of people out there, just like you, who are trying to improve their lives and find love. You aren't the only one.

When you meet a guy, give him a chance. Some people are extremely shy, so when you meet them for the first, and even the second time, you're not seeing the real person.

Personally, I root for this guy because it means he's not a player. He hasn't practiced his lines on hundreds of women before you. He likes you so much already, but he's afraid that he'll say something wrong to cause you to bolt.

The best way to manage your time with someone you've just met is to plan fun activities to do together and approach it as building a friendship, which is a solid foundation for a relationship. You don't want to become his best guy friend by sitting around, scratching yourself and watching football games while you belch the alphabet, but you can go hiking, explore a new coffee house together, go bowling or a dozen other activities that are date-like, just approach these dates as fun activities.

This allows a shy guy to let his guard down and have some fun. He's more likely to climb out of his shell if you're having fun, laughing together. It also helps you begin to build small bits of intimacy and memories. All the while, you're intriguing him with an adventurous side.

MYTH #2: Men my age aren't looking for a commitment.
You've spent time on a few dating apps, and you've met a few guys, but they all say they aren't looking for anything serious right now, so you begin to believe this is a global truth about all men.

The truth, however, might be that people are less willing to settle for someone less than their dream partner. This is not a bad thing, but they're probably articulating it in the wrong way.

Saying he isn't looking for a commitment might just mean he doesn't want you to get your hopes up until he's decided whether you fit his criteria or not.

Heck, I said that exact thing to my significant other...and yes, she reminds me of that all the time.

From the male point of view, we're clueless to the milestones you start piling up. If he kisses you or doesn't on a first date, that has much more significance to you than it does to him.

How long he waits to call or text you after a date is a *big* deal to you, but to him, it's not. He might have been busy at work, or maybe he had to take a trip or someone close to him got sick. Dozens of things could keep him from texting you back in the timeframe you feel is acceptable.

Men don't text right back unless you know how to text them in a way that motivates them. *Right back* for a man might be two hours, or it could be two days. Meanwhile, in that two hours, or two days, you've decided he's a worthless slime ball and your friends are backing you up.

Relax your dating schedule. Spend time truly getting to know one another, instead of buying a *Bride* magazine after the second date. Don't immediately look to every guy and see husband, even if marriage is part of your dream vision. This causes you to rush him, and if he feels rushed into something he's not ready for, he'll bolt.

Date to have fun. Go places. Do things together. **Build memories.** Forget the wedding plans until you're much further along in your relationship. He's dating you to have fun and learn more about you. If you date to have fun and learn more about him, you'll find yourself much happier in the long run.

MYTH #3: A great guy will accept me, even in my worst moments.

Ideally, we would always accept the person we love, no matter what happens. But the truth is some people are just not cut out to handle your worst and when it does come on, they simply don't know what to do, so they give up.

Let me tell you about Tia and Rob. They were in love. They dated for three years and decided to buy a house together. You could tell Rob loved Tia by the way he acted around her. For example, he would put his hand at the small of her back when they walked, a protective measure.

After they had dated for a year, he helped her move into a new apartment, on Valentine's Day, in a snowstorm. Two years later, they bought a house together. Even the week before she ended their relationship, he followed her home one night to pump gas for her because it was dark, and he didn't want her to do it alone.

So, what broke them up? Tia's job became very stressful. She got a new boss who was a real jerk. He would come to her workplace and berate her for an hour, over things that weren't even wrong, and she had to take that home with her.

Every workday, Tia would come home, make a margarita and crawl into a hot bath to cry in frustration. Rob didn't know what to do.

While Tia searched for a new job, the abuse at work continued and Rob began looking for someone else to love. One day, while Tia was at home, a text came through on Rob's iPad—from another woman. Devastated, Tia ended their relationship and found a new job.

It wasn't that Rob didn't love Tia. I believe he did, and his actions prove it. After she broke up with him, he was equally devastated—he knew he had hurt her deeply and he tried to apologize to her for days. Even so, he couldn't handle her worst moments, even though he loved her.

We owe the ones we love the best of what we have to offer. Could Tia have managed things differently? Perhaps. It's easy to allow our emotions to overrun us, instead of gaining control of them, but that is something many people never learn to do.

I do believe that, if you marry, you're in it for better or worse, but I also believe it's up to each of us to learn how to control our emotions so that even our worst doesn't allow us to be out of control. You *are* in control of your emotions and science tells us that when you're in a highly emotional state, you cannot think logically or rationally, so it's in your best interest to try to learn to control it.

Now, I'm not telling you to become an emotionless robot. All I'm saying is that when something happens, choose your response carefully. If you want to cry, fine, cry, but be realistic about how long you cry. Expressing yourself is a healthy thing, if you are in control of it, and you're not allowing it to control you.

MYTH #4: There is nobody like "X"—I will never find someone like him again.

This is true but let me explain this myth a little better so you can move past it.

You met a great guy. He was perfect. He was handsome. He had a great job, and when the two of you were together, things just clicked. You've never felt happier and it was all because of him.

No. It wasn't. And, you're not with him any longer, for one reason or another, so something wasn't so perfect.

You're right in saying you won't find someone like him again, instead you will find someone better. Instead of seeking his perfect twin, seek the same feelings.

Look for another man who makes you feel special, loves your quirky side and enjoys spending time with you. Don't look for another guy just like that one perfect guy. He wasn't so perfect after all or you would still be together. Look for another man who can make you feel as if you're the only woman in the room.

Look for the guy who puts his hand at the small of your back, smiles at the sight of you and makes you forget how frustrated you were just an hour before at work.

No two people are alike, but that doesn't mean you can't replicate those great feelings of being in love, and this time, with the right guy!

MYTH #5: When I find the right guy, the relationship will be easy.

This is one I've heard, over and over again, and it's time for it to go away. Great relationships are **not** easy. They take hard work. If you want easy, go to Tinder. If you want great, seek out a great man and a strong relationship, understanding that it will take hard work.

When you meet a new guy, he will bring out new things in you, and you in him. He has unique interests that he will want to share with you and, if you're adventurous enough, you'll accept his challenge.

Two people who are great for one another push each other to grow, and they grow together. They try new things, meet new people and enjoy new experiences.

Kate and John had dated for a while. They were very different people, but something drew them together. Kate loved sports while John was more of a scientist-geek. John did have his adventurous side, though, and asked Kate to join him after a business trip out west.

Even though Kate had never been hiking in the mountains before, she agreed to go and had the most phenomenal time. The hike was several hours up the mountain, and then several hours down. It was physically exhausting. She felt both wiped out and exhilarated at the end.

John had stretched her beyond anything she'd done before, and he learned to like sports. They pushed one another to try new things and to grow as individuals.

A great relationship takes hard work, patience, an adventurous spirit and the desire to be better today than you were yesterday. It takes learning how to communicate with one another, including developing the ability to truly listen.

Now, before I leave this topic, it's important to understand that there is a *good* hard and a bad hard in a relationship. When a relationship is difficult because one or both of you are toxic for one another, that's a bad kind of hard. Being in an abusive situation is the wrong kind of hard as well.

Hard is good when it's helping you grow either as an individual or as a couple. It's positive activities and positive growth.

Hard is bad when it's abusive or toxic. When one or both of you lack the confidence to build a truly interdependent relationship, versus a codependent relationship.

Being in a great relationship means you encourage one another to be better. Insecurities might creep up, but instead of cramming them back down, you face and overcome them. It's not easy to do, but it's often the best way to build a stable, happy relationship.

MYTH #6: No man wants to date or marry a successful woman like me.

This is a myth that women have been fed for years and it's time to let it go. The truth is that we attract people who are most like us.

This is good news and bad news, depending on your confidence and self-esteem levels. People with low confidence and low self-esteem tend to draw the same types of people to themselves. Whether it's relationships with the opposite sex or friends, we tend to migrate toward people most like us.

When you look at it in terms of your success, what it means is that you're more likely to date a man who has a similar education level to yours, but you're just as likely to date a man who shares your values, religion and attitudes toward different topics.

You will be the same in one of those areas, but probably not all of them.

I know that if you're a very successful woman, you probably feel you need to hide that from a man, at least for a while. The truth is that you shouldn't hide who you are, ever. Don't be ashamed of your success. The right man will appreciate the intrigue of dating a woman like you.

He might not be as successful as you, but you may meet him at church, or at a charity event and you have that in common. There are plenty of men out there to love you for who you are—the whole package—and it's best not to hide your true self from anyone. Be who you are and never lessen your success or gifts because the other person might feel intimidated. Let the chips fall where they may.

Hiding who you are just delays the ultimate demise of the relationship if he can't accept it. A confident man won't be swayed by a more successful woman if you share attitudes, religion or values.

How to stop falling for these myths

Well, ideally, I could get you to stop watching rom coms, but that's not realistic. What I can encourage you to do is remember that these relationships you see on television, in the movies and in books are idealized—they aren't real.

People had to make them up. Real relationships don't happen in the movies or on the pages of a book. They happen in real life with real people and real hearts at stake.

While it's all warm and fuzzy to see the geeky guy fall for the beautiful woman, or for the dashingly handsome guy to fall for the shy girl, despite her effort to be invisible, it's all fantasy—it's fake.

The truth is that you can find the right guy, and you're in the right place to do so. You're single and you're doing your homework on how to find a great guy. You want to do better and that means you will, if you're willing to do the work that comes along with positive change.

The remainder of this book is designed to help you do just that—make positive changes and move toward finding a great guy. It won't be easy, but there are enough great guys out there, regardless of your age. You can feel love again, even if it's with someone else, and regardless of how successful you are.

The Ultimate Key to Dating and Finding the Man of Your Dreams

While dating, you're trying to find a healthy relationship, not just any relationship. Your goal is to find someone who is good for you. In order to do that, you need to know yourself.

Having a vibrant, developed social life is the key to a great dating life. It's also the key to becoming a confident woman and it's the key to keeping the passion alive once you make the transition into a serious relationship. To sum it up, your social life is everything!

Don't get me wrong. Your confidence has roots in other areas of your life as well, like your family, your job and your education. But these things are not a social life by any means. A social life revolves around your interests and your pursuit of developing those interests with others who share them. Those people will become the nucleus of your independence and pride.

Your confidence comes from your social life!

This doesn't mean you should stop going to bars, if that's your thing. Bars are a great way to supplement your social life, but they should only be a supplement and not your entire social life. Your social life is more than meeting men, it's about developing personal pride and confidence. It's about creating a you who is totally different from anyone else.

Your social life is about confidence. You become empowered when you have things to do outside of work and dating. You will feel better about yourself because you're growing. That growth is critical to sustaining your new mindset, promoting greater self-awareness and developing more self-esteem than you can imagine. You'll have lots of endorphins dancing throughout your body!

Your social life will be your fallback during your relationship too. When things get rough—that's where you will head to gain clarity.

Now, to get This New Mindset Working for You

It's one thing to read this and sit on it. It's another thing entirely to start taking control of your life—to start acting and creating your new, authentic life. It's time to start applying what you've learned so far to beginning that new life. By the end of this book, you'll be a brand name—a recognizable, unique woman with tons of value to offer. You'll be a **Tigress** who is free to roam and find men on your terms!

Exercise 8 is a quick one you should try before you move on.

Your Inner Game

Most people don't realize they have an inner game going on—men and women alike. I see questions on the forums all the time about people who feel out of touch with themselves. They feel lost and don't know what to do in order to feel in control again. It saddens me to read how hopeless some of these folks feel.

Unfortunately, throughout your life, there are negative experiences, but hopefully, they're balanced with positive ones too. The problem with the inner game is that it's often easier to recall the negatives and ruminate on them. Positive or negative, this collection of life experiences has created the person you are today.

The great news is that you are not your past. You are a ball of clay, striving to mold yourself into a new shape. Willingness to change is an awesome first step!

Have you ever spoken to someone who likes to distort reality so they can remain seemingly miserable? People like this act as if they're not in control of their own lives. Life happens to them and there's absolutely nothing they can do to stop or prevent it.

Let's look at Meg. Meg is older now, but this behavior has been going on for her entire life. Meg creates drama by injecting her own distortions into the story. If someone doesn't reply to a text in the timeframe she thinks is acceptable, she determines that they're angry with her—and she can even create a reason as to why they're angry. Therefore, of course, Meg must be angry back because that's just how it works.

Feeling miserable is a comfortable and learned behavior for her. It's something other women in her family did as well. She sees the negatives more often than the positives. She has an undying need to be right, even in the face of the truth and she spends a lot of her time unhappy. *This is her inner game.*

The truth for Meg is that often, people aren't angry with her, they're just busy with their own lives, but by the time she comes to learn this, it's too late and she's spent days or weeks, if not years in a state of misery.

Your Inner Game

The truth of the reality we create for ourselves is that it dictates every other aspect of our lives, including relationships with the opposite sex. While I can't change the reality of your life so far, I can help you learn how to interpret your present reality and what lies ahead, simply by helping you boost your confidence and self-esteem.

Your inner game is all about your relationship with one important person—you. Before you can work on having better relationships with a man, it's crucial that you improve the relationship you have with yourself. To some extent, you've begun this work already in the workbook exercises. In this chapter, you're going to take things further.

In previous chapters and exercises, you uncovered your self-talk and started turning the negative language into positive language. This is an essential step in improving your inner game. If you skipped that exercise or breezed through that chapter, it's time to go back. This is one of the most important things you will get from this book.

It isn't just about turning around the way you talk to yourself. This is a mindset shift from a dysfunctional, unhealthy mindset to a healthy mindset that helps you get anything you want out of life.

As you work on your mindset, it's important to recognize that your thoughts are not always true reality.

Sometimes, your thoughts are fabrications or distortions of reality—myths like we talked about a little bit ago—things you believe without proof of their existence.

In Exercise 9, which you should do now, you will learn how to distinguish between what's real and what your mind has fabricated to be true.

The truth is that your actions, your responses to stimuli and your reactions to things happening around you are completely within your control. Most often, negativity is driven by fear and anxiety, which have become part of your normal, everyday life.

The good news is that you don't need to live with fear and anxiety, and in fact, it's not healthy for you to do so. Your body's chemical responses to fear and anxiety can be dangerous to your health if they're maintained over an extended period.

Your body responds to fear and anxiety by altering heart rate, blood pressure and a host of other systems, all designed to protect you from harm. Maintaining these altered states is harmful.

This brings us full circle to those negative thoughts. I told you earlier, they dominate everything. Now, you're beginning to understand just what everything means.

You are in control!

Branding Yourself for Dating

Marketing and Dating? They're Practically Synonymous

You might not be into marketing. Heck, most people aren't, but the truth is that if you want to succeed in finding a great guy, a little marketing is required.

Suppose you decide to look for Mr. Wonderful online. Online dating is a lot about marketing. It's all you have in the beginning. You're *advertising* yourself in order to find a guy. I know, it sounds wrong to say it that way, but let's look at dating for what it is.

You're putting your best foot forward in order to find a great guy. In order to do that, he needs to be able to figure out what you have to offer—how the two of you fit.

Every human being is a completely unique person. Even twins aren't the same in every single way. Your interests and passions, your collection of life experiences and your goals, when combined, make you a very distinctive, special human being. Regardless of whether those experiences are positive or negative, they make up the person you are today.

A great man will be thrilled at the opportunity to dig into your uniqueness and figure out who you are. It is those things about you, some of which you probably hate, that will intrigue him. He'll be interested in those piano lessons your parents made you take and how it helped develop your love of music. He'll be fascinated by how you can melt wax, add some scent and a wick and make it all into a candle. He can't wait to hear about the trip you took a couple years ago on the Appalachian Trail.

It's Your Uniqueness that Makes the Biggest Difference

Whether we're talking about online dating, meeting a guy in a bar or being set up by your friends, your uniqueness will win you the date with a great guy!

Think about it from your point of view for a minute. How many guys have you seen wearing the same pleated khaki slacks with cuffs, pointy shoes and button-down shirt with their hair slicked back? How many guys have approached you with some sleezy line? How many men do you see in cowboy boots, jeans and a t-shirt?

They're all the same.

How many guys do you see who are awkwardly smoothing their shirt before they approach? How many guys stumble over their words and approach cautiously? Not as many, right? They're unique, and they're probably the best guys you'll meet!

We are trained by social media and advertising to be the same. They tell us how to dress, where to hang out, which political party we should choose and whether we should eat and drink specific foods. Society tells us which cars are socially acceptable to drive, which clothing brands we should wear and what shows we should watch on television.

But I'm interested in the woman who is a little different from her friends. I am not interested in the woman who's hanging out with women in pencil skirts, blouses unbuttoned too low and overdone makeup. My type of girl has barely any makeup on and she is comfortable in nice jeans and a shirt. She has chosen to be unique—not to conform.

This girl has my interest right away because she doesn't care what her friends are wearing. She chose to be herself. I want to approach this woman. I want to learn more about her and what makes her tick.

I like her brand!

In the first chapter, you learned about uniqueness. Now, it's time to apply it to building a brand for yourself. It's time to take your uniqueness to the next level.

Define Your Dating Brand

A business brand helps you develop a relationship between you and your customer. It helps them understand who you are and what you stand for. It tells people what you want them to know about your business—it's the *story* of the business.

In dating, it's much the same, except it relates to men instead of customers. You're building your romantic brand, instead of a business brand.

Your dating brand has a few key aspects, some of which we've touched upon previously.

Your Values

Your brand must include your values because, as you already learned, values can be the equating factor for two people. If you don't align on values, things aren't going to go well.

Previously, we talked about values as they relate to happiness, and, if you did the exercise in the workbook, you spent some time uncovering your values.

When you think about your values, this subsequently leads you to what you believe, which takes you straight to your attitudes about different topics and your priorities in life.

It might seem as if adding these things to your brand makes you seem pushy or too 'out there', but a great man will appreciate that you know yourself and what you want. He knows, up front, what you value and whether the two of you have common ground.

Don't Hide **Most** *Things*

Transparency is a big buzzword these days, in business and personal affairs, but what does it mean to be transparent in dating?

Well, first of all, it doesn't mean that you tell your entire life story in one date. That's not transparency, that's a lack of confidence and boundaries.

Transparency means you don't play games and you have no hidden agenda. If you're looking for someone to do fun stuff with and you aren't looking for a husband right now, say so. If you do want to get married and settle down, show it to the world.

Too often, we build who we are around the person we're with. "*Oh, you like avocados on your salad?* **So do I!**"

Just stop it, unless you really do like avocados on your salad. Don't fake commonalities. Don't fake interest in football if you don't even know the shape of the ball. Be who you are—the genuine article. I keep saying it and I hope you believe it now—a great man will love you for your uniqueness!

Having said that, there are things you don't need to reveal right away, and those are more personal things about you, but, be yourself.

Be Aware of Your Social Media Presence

In today's social climate, if you meet someone, they're likely to stalk you a little on social media. Come on, you've done it—I know you have!

This means you need to be mindful of what you're posting online. If you come across to some new guy as all bubbly and upbeat, but he visits your Facebook page and all he sees is you complaining about your job or your ex, the incongruence will turn him away. He'll think he didn't meet the real you.

I know it's fun to dump on the world in social media, but it's important to keep in mind that bosses, as well as potential romantic partners, can see everything you write.

Be careful and mindful of what you're putting out there.

Instead of complaining or blasting people online, try showcasing your brand. Show photos of you having fun, going on adventures, traveling or pursuing your hobbies and passions. Be positive and upbeat and showcase who you are.

Let the world see the person you want to be. Let them embrace the unique and genuine you.

Care about Your Appearance

Regardless of your body type, your hair, or your preference for more or less makeup, it's important to show the world that you care about yourself. While I understand the comfort of pajamas, I cannot see the wisdom of going to the grocery store while still wearing them, and yet, I see it all the time.

I understand that sometimes, getting dressed is just more effort than it's worth and if you plan to sit at home and binge watch something on Netflix, I've got no problems with it, but if you're going out in public, show the world you care about yourself and put your best foot forward.

Now, since I can already hear you protesting that I'm being sexist, allow me to clarify.

Putting your best foot forward simply means going out in clothing that shows you respect yourself. That's not blouses unbuttoned to your belly button, skirts you can't sit down in and jeans that have so many slices in them, nobody can figure out why you bothered to put them on.

Your clothing and accessories tell the world a lot about what you think of yourself. If you dress in clothing that's too revealing, it says you don't value yourself. If you dress in the crappiest thing you own, it says you don't have any self-respect. Again, if you're sitting at home with a tub of ice cream and the Fire Stick remote, go for it, but in public, respect yourself.

Mind Your Actions

How you present yourself extends beyond your clothing, hair and makeup. It also shows up in how you act when you're out.

Fifty-five percent of our communication with others is non-verbal. This means you communicate a lot with your facial expressions and actions.

Your body language tells others a *lot* about you. For example, allowing your hair to fall over your face signals low self-esteem. Being unable to look someone in the eye is the same. Slumped shoulders and staying turned away from the room signals to others that you're unapproachable.

Use your body language to it's fullest. Drop those arms that are crossed over your chest, square your shoulders and face the room. Smile more. Don't be afraid to make eye contact for a few seconds before looking away. If you want him to know you're interested, look back after a few seconds, then look away again.

All these things tell a great guy he can approach. These signals are key to that shy guy who is trying to get up the nerve to come talk to you.

Passions—Again

I bet you thought I was done talking about your passions, but they fit into your brand, so here we go again! Don't be afraid to share your passions with others. Wear that Habitat for Humanity t-shirt to the grocery store. Put on your

Patriots jersey on game days. Find a tee or some other item that represents your passion for animals.

I'm not saying that every time you leave your house, you need to be wearing something like that, but don't be afraid to showcase who you are.

What Value can You Bring to HIS Life?

In business, it's all about solving a customer's problems—bringing value, but value comes in all shapes and sizes. For a luxury automobile, the value to the customer is in the status, not in simply owning a car. They can get that value by buying any vehicle.

What uniqueness, what value, can you bring to a man's life? How are you different from the ten other women he can see right now? What sets you apart?

When a man meets you, or vice versa, the question at some point will be, *"What can this person add to my life?"* I know it sounds kind of shallow, but it's true.

I know you're special and hopefully, soon you will know you're special too. The point of this section is to make sure you let others know you're special!

In Exercise 10, you can begin building your brand.

Communicating Your Brand

In Exercise 10 of your workbook, you worked on your story and tagline. If you haven't completed those, head over and do them before reading on. Don't worry, I'll wait!

Immediately after the first two activities is the opportunity to recall stories from your past that relate to the tagline terms you wrote down. This is an equally important step because communicating your brand happens in three ways.

Go ahead and do the writing activity.

Writing About Yourself

If you choose online dating, you will be asked to write a profile and provide a headline or tagline. You just developed your tagline in the last exercise. You can use pieces from the story you wrote in the first part of the exercise to develop your description.

Notice I didn't say to write a list. Don't write a list. Write a story that focuses on those three items you've uncovered. People relate to stories. Don't make your story about Debbie Downer. Make it positive and upbeat. Highlight those unique things that make you who you are.

As you get emails from men, be sure to weave those tagline terms in, as they are part of the fabric of who you are. Own that tagline because it represents three key aspects of who you are.

Verbal Communication

When you meet a man, whether it's online or in person, you will eventually have a verbal conversation, not a written one. As you make those tagline terms more a part of your daily mindset, you will be able to use them in verbal communication. If your personality word was funny, be funny. If it was outgoing, be outgoing.

Knowing who you are helps you be confident in your communication with men.

My brand is being funny. I know it, I practice it, and I deliver it when I am with people!

You can also use the stories you wrote in Exercise 10—those stories about your past that communicate those tagline terms. People learn about you through your stories. Men enjoy hearing about the time you went to Aruba on Spring Break with your friends or the time you took a vacation without making any reservations ahead of time.

They like hearing about your childhood dog, Ralph, who was your best friend before you went to school or about the time in college that you and your friends decided to go visit a nursing home and play games with the residents.

Stories are inroads to our lives, and they give people a better idea of who you are than any other thing you can do.

Non-Verbal Communication

I just touched on body language a little while back, and this is non-verbal communication. So much of your communication happens without you even recognizing it, but if you take the time to become aware of your body language and the messages you're sending out into the world, you will be surprised at the changes.

Ask a trusted friend about your body language and ask them to help you improve. Your best friend can easily text you from across the room, "Hey Jen, unfold your arms" and it will make a big difference! Help each other!

And Now...to Target the Right Type of Man

In business, it's important to define your niche—that segment of the larger market you can target for advertising. The same goes for dating. While you might enter dating thinking you want any guy, the truth is that there is a *particular type of guy* who is right for you.

Whether you're creating an online profile or just going out to hang with your friends, it's important to know the characteristics of this guy ahead of time.

Luckily for you, there is another activity in your workbook (Exercise 10 What's Your Type of Guy) to help you with this.

Let's imagine you put up an online profile that doesn't specify any preferences in a man. You don't specify height, body type, education level, career, ethnicity or anything.

The first ten guys who respond are all wrong. Two are too short. One has a body type you're not interested in. One is in a career you just don't want to deal with, three don't have the education level you prefer, and the rest are of an ethnicity you would rather not date.

All ten emails were a waste of your time, and theirs.

This is why it's so important to be specific. If some of those things don't matter to you, fine, but I bet some do.

Building Your Brand

While completing these steps to build your brand can seem tedious at times, and maybe make you feel a bit uncomfortable, it's an important step.

The more time, thought and energy you put into it, the stronger your brand will be when you're done. The better you will know yourself and the more likely you will be to find and keep a great guy! If you haven't noticed, this chapter is helping you get to know yourself and understand aspects of your dating life that you might not have given much thought to before.

The most important result of building your brand is that your dating confidence, as well as your confidence in general, will begin to improve. You will begin to see that your uniqueness isn't a negative, it's a positive. The negative things you thought about yourself are not true. All those negative things you say to yourself are beginning to go away and you're starting to see the wonderful woman other people see.

Plotting the Course

Your first task in building your confidence is to start asking yourself a lot of deep questions. Of course, you've already been answering a lot of questions in just these first few chapters, so you might be wondering what else there is to ask.

Ask questions to explore who you are. Have you ever asked yourself any of the questions you've found in this book or the workbook?

Sure, you might not like some of the answers but that's okay. The answers give you a baseline to start thinking about the upcoming changes. Some questions are easier to answer than others. The answer to, "What is my life's passion?" may be easy for some and impossible for others.

I'm assuming you've thought about this. You'd love to have things to do outside of work or school, but you have no idea what. Even worse, you may be under the assumption that you're weird because you don't have a passion or interest. If this is you, drop that thought! It's normal to be where you are.

I know you've spent time on passions already, but before you press on, I want to clarify a few things.

Passions are NOT

Unless you get lucky, your passion is not something you'll just happen to come across randomly. Passions aren't just sitting in your head, waiting impatiently for you to take them up. For example, you may find you're passionate about playing the violin if you try it, but if you never try, you'll never know.

You will have to work to find your passion. If it was so easy, everyone would already be doing it.

Some get luckier than others when seeking their passions. I wasn't always a dating coach, nor had the thought really crossed my mind until a friend of mine suggested I start a website. One thing led to another and now I'm happily engaged in writing books and helping women build dating confidence. I've always loved the art of dating, but I never thought it would turn out this way.

Passions are just pastimes that engage you and make you happy. You want to find something that challenges you and helps you grow. Something that's *just fun* won't do that.

Most people will die having never pursued or found their passion.

Don't get down on yourself if you try something and it doesn't pan out. It may take a lot of different tries to find things that interest you. Your job right now is to get motivated to find the thing that challenges you!

Even if you're 70, it's not too late to uncover your passion!

And remember, people have many passions—they just haven't found them yet!

How do You Find These Interests?

Finding your passions and interests will take some effort but there are a lot of men and women who are looking at the same time you are. In fact, it's never been easier to use the Internet as a platform to find people with similar interests or get ideas for what might interest you.

If you're worried about being too shy to be part of a new group, I've got two words for you: **(wo)man up!** You may not be confident yet, but gaining confidence is all about putting yourself out there.

Are you reading this just to read another dating book or are you in it to make real changes in your dating life? My guess is you want to make real changes and that begins by meeting new people and going out of your comfort zone.

In order to avoid becoming overwhelmed, don't try everything at once. You have all the time in the world to work on this. It's a never-ending process of searching for interests and improving upon them. Don't try to be Speedy Gonzales. Just keep things simple and don't overwhelm yourself.

This is the biggest problem people face when they start looking for a new interest—they take too much in all at once and give up because they spend too much time daydreaming about the result. The problem with this line of thinking is that there **is no result**.

You are ultimately seeking a change in mindset. You're pursuing interests to develop a happier, more valuable life. There is no end to this, it's a lifelong pursuit.

Oh, and this happens to be where you will find your great guy!

One way to narrow it down is to brainstorm some areas in which you might find passion. Take ten minutes and make a list, then sleep on it, and review the list. Which five rise to the top? Choose one and go after it. If it doesn't turn out to be a true passion, move on to the next.

Developing your personal brand means you need to start getting out there and making things happen. Yes, you can write lists of things that potentially interest you but if that's all you do, you'll go nowhere. You need to look for and **try** ideas. They won't just plop into your head like magic.

The more you search for ideas and the more you pursue interests, the more confidence you will build and the easier it becomes. Once you build your confidence, your true personality traits will start shining through stronger than ever before. Personality is a big part of your brand, but it isn't always easy to express when you're shy or uncomfortable.

Last year, I met a woman named Jen who was very sweet and shy. As I got to know her, I could see she had a wild side and an interest in my motorcycle. Motorcycles carry that

I'm wild and free image, so I suggested she learn how to ride a bike. She resisted at first but then followed through. Today, Jen owns a bike and has new friends, one of whom is her new boyfriend. Her brand is not sweet and shy any more, it's outgoing and rebellious. She wouldn't have figured this out if she didn't stir the pot and try something new.

What might have happened to Jen? Some dominant man could have entered her life and molded her into someone she isn't because she didn't know what her interests were. This sweet shy girl wouldn't have discovered who she really is and what she really enjoys in life. This is how relationships fail. This is why people stumble through life unhappy.

Why All of this Matters to Your Dating Life

Being able to fall back on your interests and passions will save you from a lot of heartbreak in the future. Women who don't have passions either go straight into another bad relationship or they dig their heels into their career and leave the dating game, potentially forever. Neither of these scenarios is probably part of your dream. Both are preventable with solid interests you can use to get your mind off men when the worst happens.

Having hobbies when you're dating is an incredible way of keeping things interesting and this is even truer when you're in a relationship. You can really throw a man off when you have an active social life. Men love it when a woman has a social life that doesn't revolve around them. Furthermore, you will avoid the jealous types who want their partner home and not part of any social circle.

With an outside life, you're not predictable, and this is one key to a strong relationship.

Now It's Time

If you got anything out of this chapter, I hope it's that you are a true believer in the art of branding yourself. When you develop a distinct brand that you can be proud of, everything in your life realigns, including the kind of men you meet.

When you have your own brand, you have more control over your life and a stronger appreciation for who you are. **You get exposure to descent men**. You have stronger relationships that are capable of surviving over time. The type of woman you are determines what kind of man is good for you. The less you know yourself, the less likely you are to make an informed decision about finding the guy who is right for you.

Just like everything else that has this much value in your life, it won't develop overnight. Take your time. Start seeking potential interests and when you feel overwhelmed, back off. Pick it up the next day if you need to but never stop searching until you find something. Once you do, never stop challenging yourself because when you aren't challenged, you won't grow.

Unlocking the Power of Gratitude

Gratitude. You've most likely heard of this time and time again. It's easily one of the most important words in the English language and a concept essential to living a fulfilled life.

Most people, however, practice gratitude incorrectly (notice the word practice). When life is amazing, they practice gratitude and are thankful, they have abundance and they are inspired. When life throws them challenges, they are negative, constricted and play the victim game. We've all been there, right?

Authentic gratitude comes when you can accept positive and negative, success and failure, opportunity and obstacle, pleasure and pain. Life is not a one-sided game. There are polarities at every extreme. That's another universal law, but what does it mean? It means:

- *There's no light without dark*
- *There's no pleasure without pain*
- *There's no love without fear*

While this is a short chapter, it's an important one, and in your workbook, Exercise 11 can help you further.

The power of gratitude brings a change of perspective. I was once driving down the highway in Los Angeles and, of course, there was bumper-to-bumper traffic. I was stressed, late to a meeting and starving, not to mention dehydrated. Never a good combination. The entire ride was a junkyard of negativity, yelling at strangers and at myself and blaming others. Then I remembered a quote from a podcast I had been listening to a while back:

"Your biggest complaint right now would be someone else's amazing dream luxury."

It completely blew me away and changed my entire frame of mind at that moment.

The truth is that there is a lot of value in practicing gratitude in your everyday life. People who do so find themselves suffering less from depression and they're happier.

When you're focused on the good things that have come to you in your life, you're not focusing on the bad. Tricky, right?

Maybe, but it's so powerful that you just can't avoid it. Personally, I write five gratitude statements every day, and I work very hard not to repeat anything. Yes, some days I am grateful for warm socks or not stubbing my toe on my bureau, but it doesn't matter. The point is to be grateful for the things that went well.

Benefits of Gratitude

People who keep a journal of things and people they're grateful for have a higher level of satisfaction with their live, according to a **National Institute of Health (NIH) study**. **Other studies** show the following benefits of gratitude.

Improved Sleep

When you're counting your blessings, instead of being weighed down by the negatives of the day, it helps you rest more peacefully and even get to sleep faster. Therefore, the best time of day to practice gratitude might be right before you go to bed.

Improved Impulse Control

Impulse control spans several areas of our lives, not the least of which is overeating. When you practice impulse control, you slow down your decision making and are less likely to make impulsive decisions, like a piece of cake instead of an apple or that pair of shoes instead of saving for vacation.

Lower Instances of Feeling Depressed

Gratitude has been shown to help patients who suffer from depression. It often performs better than drugs people use for the same thing.

Lasting Happiness

I suppose lasting happiness and lower levels of depression kind of go together. Happiness comes from focusing on the good things happening in your life. While instant gratification from that piece of cake or new pair of shoes goes away rather quickly, feeling grateful for the money to buy those shoes will last you longer.

Better Appreciation for Your Body

When people practice gratitude, science tells us that they are more likely to engage in healthy eating habits, exercise and other self-care activities. You just feel more like going to the gym when you're practicing gratitude daily.

Patience isn't a Virtue, it's a Product of Gratitude

When you're grateful, you're also more patient and better able to make good decisions. Part of this might come from the fact that when you're feeling less emotional, you're able to make more logical decisions. Your mind cannot handle heavy emotions and big decision-making events at the same time.

Long-Lasting Relationships

I've seen this in many studies. Couples who have been happily married for many years often report that one thing they practiced was gratitude. Not only are they grateful for things in their lives, but they focus on being grateful for their partner and what he or she brings to their lives.

Feeling Connected during Times of Crisis

When you practice gratitude and you experience a crisis or significant loss, you're more likely to trudge through it with a sense of being connected and not alone. This helps you navigate the crisis and enables you to focus on positives.

Practicing Gratitude Daily

So, you know it's beneficial to be grateful, now it's time to learn how to go about it.

Keep a Gratitude Journal

This is the easiest way to maintain a practice of gratitude. Earlier, you learned that if you write your gratitude statements before bed, you're more likely to sleep well. Keep your journal by your bedside and make it part of your bedtime routine to write 3-5 statements of gratitude each night.

Take a Few Minutes to Meditate

Sometimes, the day can be hectic, but if you take a few minutes to close your eyes, breathe deeply and practice a little gratitude, everything can even out. Stop, close your eyes, breathe deeply and ask yourself what you're grateful for. Really allow this feeling to flow through you and enjoy it. If you want to ramp up your feeling, visualize your gratitude.

Let Others Know

It's not just good manners to say "Thank You" often, it's a great practice of gratitude, if, of course, you mean it. When someone, stranger or not, opens a door or does something else kind for you, say "Thank You". I like to make sure I thank military people I see when I'm out and about. I also buy them coffee or lunch.

Stay Out of the Complaining Zone

It's easy to get caught up in someone else's complaining, but this takes away from your happiness as well. Instead, kindly excuse yourself from the conversation. Find a quiet place where you can take a couple of minutes to do that meditation gratitude thing you just learned.

Write a Letter

If someone has done something particularly kind for you, write them a letter expressing your gratitude. If possible, give it to them in person. This not only helps you focus on positives, but everyone loves to be appreciated for their kindness.

Be Grateful for You

Take some time, every now and then, to be grateful for you. What have you done to improve yourself? Maybe reading this book or going to work out. Perhaps you've decided to practice self-care every morning or you've taken on a volunteer position somewhere. Whatever it is, be grateful for your own positives and reward yourself!

Exercise 11 in your workbook will help you get started with gratitude!

Making the Right First Impression

I know, it's cliché to say it, but you never get a second chance to make a first impression. The truth of falling in love with someone is that the first impression is something many never forget. You'll hear elderly couples telling you what the other wore the first time they met, maybe more than 60 years earlier.

First impressions matter. Is it possible to meet Mr. Wonderful when you're running around in your grubby sweats, leaves in your hair and no makeup? It can happen, sure, but the more likely time he'll notice you is when you're wearing lipstick.

Huh?

We'll circle back to that in a minute. The truth is that there are things men notice about women when they first see them. If you know me at all, you know I make no apologies for my gender. Men are animals. I can't state it any differently. We're animals. Ultimately, when we choose a woman, we *do* go for things like values and all that other stuff, but when it comes to first impressions...well, it is what it is.

I spend a lot of time trying to help you understand how the male mind operates. Women often give us too much credit for thinking things through, often because you *do* think things through and expect we are the same. This leads to frustration on your end.

Men and women don't do many things in the same way when it comes to relationships. That's probably why the divorce rate is high and why around 50% of all Americans are single. The sooner you come to accept this first truth, the easier your dating and relationship life will become.

Men are Visual

Don't shoot the messenger, but men are visual. We are constantly looking around a room for the attractive woman. This is evolutionary as it turns out. The caveman, who spent the most time looking about the seaside for the most attractive, most 'able to carry his babies' woman, survived while the ones who banged the first cavewoman they saw eventually died off. I know, you think some of them still hang around...those men today are called players.

This is evolutionary because when the caveman found the cavewoman attractive, he was more inclined to want to mate with her, thus sending his genetic code a little further down the line. He chose a woman with broader hips and one who seemed more likely to successfully conceive. Meanwhile, the lesser caveman humped every woman he saw but somehow managed not to impregnate any of them.

What this means to you is men are always looking but that doesn't mean they want to buy. So many women get jealous over the wandering eye of their man. Stop it. He's just window shopping. Much like you're just looking at those $500 pumps in the shoe store window, he's just looking. It also means that the odds of a man looking your way any time you're out and about are pretty good, yet you're probably oblivious to most of them.

Therefore, in order to be seen, you need to make yourself *available*. Let me explain. What I mean by this is don't sit in the back row of a book club you've joined, you know—to meet new people. Don't hide behind the wall divider at social events, hoping to go unnoticed. Mr. Right won't find you there. Put yourself in view of other men. Don't use your sunglasses or hat as a smokescreen either. We want to see your beautiful eyes. Let me see you. Get exposure. That's your first lesson!

What is Attractive?

Good news. No two men define attractive in the same way. Yes, some men want the tall blonde with the deep blue eyes, but some men prefer a woman who is a little heavier or one with short brunette hair. For some men, it's the smile or legs. Every man is different in what he feels is attractive. This is good news to every woman because, as luck would have it, you're all different!

So, yes, men are looking for *attractive* women, but each man's definition of attractive is different. It's like in the movie, *White Christmas*, when the two fellas go to listen to the two sisters sing for the first time. One makes mention of "her blue eyes" while the other is ogling over "her brown eyes", then they realize they're both looking at a different sister, finding them both attractive.

There are studies which indicate that our definition of attractiveness has roots in our childhood. If a man had a close relationship with his mother, and she wore a specific perfume, he will be drawn to that perfume. If she wore her hair a certain way, he might be attracted to a woman with a similar hairstyle. Word has it that Conrad Hilton found his wife by her red hat, which he saw a few rows ahead of him in church one Sunday. He followed that red hat until he met the woman beneath it and eventually married her. Probably because someone he loved in his childhood wore a red hat.

Yes, I know the beauty of individuals is more than skin deep, but that's what dating is for. We're talking about attraction right here and you can't dig that deep staring across the tomatoes at Mr. Wonderful.

What Else do Men "Look" At?

When it comes to first glances, a lot happens in a short amount of time. Let's imagine your target guy is hanging out next to the piano bar. He's spotted you and he's spotted another female. You've got that down-home, earthy look going on. Relaxed but classy. The other woman is wearing spike heels, has her hair pulled up tight into a bun and is wearing expensive-looking business attire. He may choose you over her if he feels intimidated by the more powerful looking woman. It may make him feel as if he would be sexually inadequate with her.

Now, on the other hand, if your target is into the high-power woman, she may win out in the game you don't even know you're playing. Again, it's all in what he finds attractive. Men are always screening, maybe not even consciously. "Will she be able to carry my children?" This could translate into things like her body shape—something he may not even realize he's considering.

Facial beauty, again in the eye of the beholder, is often associated with grace, intelligence and popularity. If he finds your face attractive, he will associate those qualities with you before he knows who you are inside.

In Exercise 12, you can work more on understanding attractiveness and first impressions.

10

How to Know Which Guys are the Good Guys

Rarely will a man sit down to talk to you and then say, *"Amy, you're not really my type of woman, but I'll keep you around until someone better comes along",* or, *"I'm really sorry Rachel, but I'm emotionally unavailable and incapable of loving anyone right now, but my words will convince you otherwise."*

It would be nice if we could do that, both men and women, but we don't. Mostly because we don't want to hurt someone's feelings, but players won't say it either.

So, how do you know? Well, I thought I would adapt a little bit of my book, *Weed Out the Users, the Couch Potatoes and the Losers* and present it to you here.

The User

This man is best summarized as a con artist. At first, he will show you all the signs of Mr. Right. He will socially announce you prior to getting what he wants, be enthusiastic when he is with you, and he might even meet your friends and family.

But he is a wolf in sheep's clothing. After he gets what he wants, he will quickly turn into the wolf and all his Mr. Right-ish actions will disappear. Sometimes he acts gradually, and other times he acts so quickly you don't see it coming.

I'm sure you have already dated one of these slime balls. He is the first one to walk up to you at a bar. He can be very attractive and he's usually smooth with the lines. The user can adapt like a chameleon to what he knows you like, thus giving himself every advantage required to reel you in like a spider web pulls in a fly. He oozes confidence and uses it for his own gain—but he is not confident at all, as we will soon discover.

Mr. Right, on the other hand, uses his confidence to help others and attract a long-term partner. Once the user gets your number, he pounces. He plans nighttime dates where the booze flows and your schedule is open the next day. He might plan to meet somewhere close to his house for his own convenience. He comes in other forms too. For instance, he might be online pretending to be someone he's not.

The User's Patterns of Behavior

He makes a great first impression.
Most users have confidence in their ability to pick you up. Of course, all this really means is that they are skilled in the art of the pick-up. Conversation, humor, reading you and dressing to impress are all common attributes. He's almost too good to be true. He smells good, he buys drinks for you and your friends and he looks deep into your eyes.

He listens.
Now tell me, **what guy listens???**

People get good at things by practicing them. This should tell you that you're not his first conquest and you won't be his last. This type of guy knows women and he knows how to trigger your endorphins so you'll get excited and think with your heart, instead of your head.

He comes on strong.
Users don't waste any time. On the contrary! A user is very efficient in his methodology. His one goal is to extract something from you—usually sex or money. He will scan the room, looking for the weakest women he can find, choose one and pounce.

If he meets resistance in the form of confidence, he'll retreat quickly. Nothing to see or do here. Just like a wild cat in Africa, he scans the room for his prey, but if he makes a mistake, he will turn tail and bolt. If he takes on a confident woman, he might be exposed and that's the last thing he wants!

For the pick-up artist or user, dating is a numbers game. He's addicted to the chase. This type of guy lacks confidence, even though he comes off as being incredibly confident. He validates himself by the number of women he can have sex with. Some women do the same thing.

This guy is everything you want a guy to be. He texts you, maybe before you even get home, and he will be anxious to set up another date with you. This will make you think he's really into you, but in truth, he's pushing for that validation—sex.

His questions will be self-serving.
A user or player will ask questions which help him determine whether you're a good target for him or not. He'll ask about your work schedule so he knows when he can get laid. If there are guys in your group, he'll ask about them to make sure they aren't a threat to him.

If he's interested in your money, he'll ask about your career and living situation. If he wants to glom off your status, he'll be interested in the value of what you own—your car, your home and so on.

The date will most likely be on a weekend.
To maintain efficiency, he'll plan a date on a weekend or on the evening before you have a day off. He wants to be able to take you out and fill you with booze, so your inhibitions are lowered. The date will also be near his home because he's lazy. The less work he needs to do, the better for him. And it is all about what's best for him, make no mistake about that.

He will call at the last minute.
Chances are, you're not the first girl he's asked out tonight. You're probably the third or fourth, maybe more. He has several women on the hook right now and he's simply running through the list of available women to see who he can have sex with tonight.

Your best option, as I've told you before, is to stay busy with your hobbies, friends and passions. I recommend that you don't accept a last-minute date unless it's truly something you want to do like a sports event or a concert. A man who calls you at the last minute thinks you have nothing better to do than date him.

When you say no, a great guy will try harder to be important enough to get a yes, but a user will move on and that's a good thing.

He pulls a disappearing act.
Great guys don't do disappearing acts, they want to be in your life. A user will disappear for a while, probably because he's found another target who interests him more for the moment. When he gets bored with her, he'll be back if he doesn't have anyone else.

It only takes a few seconds to shoot someone a text to let them know you're tied up with something, but it takes being courteous to do so. A man who cares about you will take the time to send that text. A user or player doesn't care about you, regardless of what he says, and being courteous is low on his list.

He leaves his online dating profile up.
When you're first dating, this isn't a red flag. You shouldn't take your profile down either until you're in a committed relationship and you shouldn't expect a man to do so either. In fact, it's perfectly acceptable for you to continue dating multiple men until one begins to show himself to be the real deal.

A player will give up on you if you're doing this. A great guy will work hard to win because men love to compete, but they also love to win! Players don't have that same belief in themselves to think they can compete or win, so they'll drop out of the race and keep surfing for easier women.

He lives up to his user status.
Users want favors from you, but don't ask them for anything. He might want to borrow money, your car or any number of things from you, but if you even think about asking him to take you to the airport, drive you home from getting your oil changed or even just open your car door for you, forget it. It's all about him, not you.

His body language says it all.
The body language of a user speaks to his low confidence. He won't make eye contact with you unless you're talking about something that interests him, like sex, status or money.

When a man is interested in you, he will square his shoulders toward you. A player will be facing the room, not you.

A player will have low concentration for anything other than topics that relate to him. When you're talking about him, he's all in, but if you manage to steer the conversation to yourself for a minute or two, he'll dial out.

Speaking of conversation, he'll keep the topic related to him or things he's interested in and if it shifts to you, he'll find a way to get back to him. He is his own favorite topic.

As he's talking about himself, he'll speak quickly. He has so much to say about himself that he needs to talk fast to cram it all in before you figure out he's a loser and you bolt. He isn't interested in your point of view on anything because he's always right.

It the beginning, he might not act this way because he knows he needs to suck you into his lair. It's only after you've seen him a couple of times that these behaviors will truly begin to appear.

He is the king of excuses.
The player has a litany of excuses:

- Sure, he'll meet you and your friends for lunch.... but he is a no-show
- He'll have an excuse that will make you feel guilty when he doesn't reach out to you after a few days
- He'll say he's going to pay you back, but you never see the money—you just hear excuses
- Once he's had his orgasm, he's done, whether you were able to climax or not, and he really doesn't

care, but he'll say he does and promise to do better next time...he won't
- Oh gosh, he forgot his wallet for this date, if you get this one, he can get the next...but he won't

A user always has an excuse for his bad behavior and it's an excuse to make you feel badly when you were right all along. He's a master liar and uses his collection of lies to keep you interested and in his bed. If he's a master player, he'll keep small promises but blow big ones.

He doesn't make plans or remember important dates.
Your birthday? He could care less. His birthday—you'd better be excited to celebrate! Don't expect him to even remember it's your birthday, let alone celebrate it. He doesn't even care how this makes you feel—he's indifferent to your feelings because he's so wrapped up in his own feelings.

He will most likely be busy on the days when you've got something important going on. He doesn't want to meet your friends or family because they might see the real him.

He's not around in the morning.
A player won't stay around for morning coffee or, for that matter, morning anything. He's more likely to leave in the middle of the night or very early in the morning. This has nothing to do with the walk of shame and everything to do with not being interested in spending quality time with anyone but himself.

He got what he wanted from you—sex—and now, he's done with you until the next time. He doesn't want to deal with your emotions and he most definitely doesn't want to snuggle or cuddle. He's not ever going to want to *talk*, unless, of course, you want to talk about him, then he's all in.

Sticking around might make him vulnerable to being discovered. He's not interested in that at all.

Having said all that, some players *will* stick around until morning, at least for a while, because it's a fun part of the game for them. Maybe he'll get more sex out of it if he hangs out.

He would rather stay in than go out.

In the beginning, you went out, but now, he just wants to hang out at his house. This not only protects his wallet, but it allows him to be able to have sex with you easier. He's selfish and cheap so he's not going to do anything to jeopardize those values.

He might make big plans with you to do things out of the house, but they never materialize and if you ask him about these plans, he'll have tons of excuses to back up his unwillingness to follow through.

He's not interested in your bad days.

A user is not even remotely interested in being around you when you're dealing with anything negative. If you're going to do something fun and the opportunity for sex is high, he's all in, but if you just lost your job, your dog died or your good friend was just diagnosed with cancer, he's going to find somewhere else to be.

Even things like moving, needing a ride to the airport or meeting your friends for lunch are immediate no's. This doesn't mean he won't ask you to do those things for him—he will—but he isn't going to do them for you.

He doesn't introduce you to the important people in his life.
A guy who is into you will want to have you meet his friends and family, over time. A user has no such interest in weaving you into his life. A man who is really into you will be excited to show you off to everyone.

Since the user knows you won't be in his life for long, he isn't interested in having his friends and family come to like you. In fact, they might even warn you off him and he surely doesn't want that!

Being with him has major ups and downs.
A user might woo you and really show you how great he can be one day, but the next day, he's MIA and you're wondering what *you* did wrong. You didn't do anything. He's just playing with you when things are going well—making an attempt to keep you around a while longer.

As soon as he returns from being MIA, he'll act like nothing happened. Everything is hunky dory and because he's convinced you that he's a great guy, you buy into his excuses and are all warm and fuzzy again when he shows up.

A great guy won't play with you like this. Your relationship with a great guy will be on a continuous upward trajectory. There might be a few small hiccups along the way, but he won't go MIA on you for days at a time.

You Can't Fix a User

I know your nurturing nature encourages you to try to fix this guy. If you can just get your claws into him, you can straighten him out. Give up on this line of thinking right now because you can't change anyone but yourself. Period. As soon as you figure out that you've snagged this type of guy, you need to let him go.

I know it won't be fun to admit you've been taken in by a user, but better to cut your losses as soon as possible, rather than get sucked in and hurt worse later.

Most men can't find their way out of this behavior, but some can. In a little bit, you'll learn about Mr. Right and then, you'll be able to recognize him easily.

Exposing the User

Your best defense is a great offense. When you start seeing someone new, don't let your heart get involved too early. Men date to have fun and you should too. In fact, this isn't the first time you've read that. Remember what I said. Have fun getting to know him.

Work hard to check your emotions and not let them get the better of you too soon. When you're first dating someone new, you're not in a relationship, you're trying each other on for size to see if a relationship makes sense for you later. Let him prove to you with his actions, and not his words, that he's into you.

Tell yourself to date with your head and not your heart, at least for the first month you're dating someone new. Within that time frame, a player will have shown his true colors.

You now know the signals and you should be keeping them in mind as you date a new guy. Don't be hypervigilant, to the point of screening all men out, but keep your eyes open and your heart uninvolved.

Pay attention to his approach.
You've already learned about this to some extent. A guy whose lines are too smooth and polished is already throwing up some red flags. The guy who stumbles over his words is not as practiced and shows more promise for being a potential great guy.

Take a trip to the ladies' room and watch.
Excuse yourself to the ladies' room and then spy on him a little. Is he approaching another woman or is he sitting there, patiently waiting for you to return? You can learn a lot by just observing him.

Don't give him your number, but get his.
He will ask you for your phone number at some point, but don't give it to him. Instead, ask him for his number. This is a boundary you should set for any new guy in your life. It's

a great test because a great guy will respect this boundary, but a user won't. The user wants to be in control of the next move, he doesn't want you to have that control.

Tell him no when he suggests a next date, then suggest your own time and place.
A user wants to maintain control of when and where you see him next. A great guy will be all in if you want to set the next date.

Your life should be full of activities relating to your friends, hobbies and passions anyway, so saying no to his suggestion shouldn't be too hard—you should have plans.

A great guy will work harder to become a priority in your life. A user will keep looking for someone who will allow him to be in control.

Don't drink much, if at all, on a first date.
The user wants to lower your inhibitions so you're easier to get in the sack. A great guy doesn't want you to be sloppy drunk because he genuinely wants to get to know you.

Keep your wits about you and mind your alcohol intake so you can continue to see the guy across the table from you for who he is, for better or worse.

Propose a daytime date.
The user wants to get into your pants on every date. To test the intentions of a new guy, ask him to meet you for brunch or lunch. A daytime date holds much less opportunity for

sex and a user knows this. He's not inclined to accept this timeframe for a date. It doesn't suit his needs. It's more likely that he can't get what he wants from you at a lunch date.

The Loser

The loser and the couch potato can be one in the same. The loser is harder to detect. He thinks he wants a relationship, but he's got stuff from his past that is preventing him from being successful in a long-term relationship.

This type of guy is unable to make a real commitment, but he may want to and it's that desire that will pull you in. At some point, you can't figure out whether the loser is making your life better or worse. Some days, he's exactly what you need, but if things get too close to real commitment, he's likely to get squeamish and pull a brief disappearing act.

This guy doesn't mean to hurt you. He wants to be in a relationship with you, but he's scared to death and can't really follow through. It's possible to marry a loser, but in the end, it won't work out. The loser will not change his behavior and the patterns of behavior you're about to read will not go away.

The Loser's Patterns of Behavior

He keeps you waiting.
This guy is a master manipulator. He knows how to stretch out time and keep giving you just enough hope to make you happy. I get the most emails from women who date losers. They share with me basically the same story, time after time. It's about a guy who keeps making promises of commitment but, year after year, nothing happens.

You think he'll come around—something will change—but nothing ever does. This is because the root of his inability to commit to you has never been addressed. Whatever turned him into a man who fears commitment still lies beneath the surface, driving his relationship actions.

He tends to be lazy and selfish.
A loser isn't often into personal growth. It might cause him to examine a painful past, which makes him uncomfortable, so he avoids it. He's not interested in meeting your friends and family and as time passes and he becomes more and more uncomfortable in the relationship, he will retreat to his friends and hobbies, leaving you standing by yourself.

He may be great in bed or have a great sense of humor—a trait that pulled you to him in the beginning, but you see less and less of it as time goes by. At some point, you'll have to work hard to get him to meet you halfway.

A great guy will be excited to meet your friends and family and to engage in activities you enjoy. He will be all about personal growth and will encourage your growth as well.

His ex may still be around.
He never really got over his ex and he keeps in close contact with her. I understand this when there are kids involved, but otherwise, there is no need for him to remain so close to her, unless, of course, he's leaving his options open. He may talk about her often, defend her actions and keep things that remind him of her nearby.

A great guy can handle his past and move forward, without clinging to someone who is gone from his life. He dates one woman at a time and doesn't care about having other options. He's into you and you alone.

Sex and affection start to slowly disappear.
At first, he's all into you. He's attentive and the sex is great, but as time passes, this guy loses the desire to play along. This is confusing to you because things were so great and then, BAM, no sex, or sex maybe once a month. This is when you know your guy is a loser and it's time to move on!

His other girlfriend is porn videos.
This guy would rather get sex without a commitment and his lazy side prefers porn. If he's not having sex with you, he's getting a release in some other way. Check his browser history and see what you find. Even if you don't find it, it could be because he's using "Private" or "Incognito" browsers.

You and your relationship with him becomes an afterthought.
At first, he paid attention to you and he was great, but now, you're last on his priority list. He's much better tuned into his own needs and the needs of his friends and family. He may even start blaming you for his own failures and issues. He knows where you're vulnerable and he uses that to make you feel as badly as he does. He makes it seem as if the failure of your relationship is your fault, not his.

Women write to me all the time and ask what they can do to fix a relationship like this. The answer is that you can't fix it—you didn't break it. Yes, you're guilty of falling for a loser, but beyond that, this is all on him. Your only way to move forward is to do so without this schmuck.

He goes MIA.
We don't need to repeat the MIA section, but you should know that a loser goes MIA just like a user does. When the relationship starts to feel too real, he's going to bolt and *if* he communicates with you, it will be to tell you that it's all your fault.

This is the point at which you say goodbye and look for a great guy instead! When he communicates with you again, and he will, ignore him—block him even—and move on. This is a pattern of behavior he will keep repeating with you for years and years if you allow him to.

If you can get him to a social event, he'll disappear.
Chances are, if you can get this guy to go to a social event with you, one of two things will happen. He will leave you to go chase another woman, or he will leave you and find a place to seclude himself from everyone. Which he chooses will depend on how many people he knows there and how well you're managing on your own.

As strange as it seems, he may be more likely to seclude himself if he knows people there than if he knows nobody. He's more comfortable hunting when he's among strangers.

He is the master at stringing you along.
I know a guy who bought an engagement ring, with absolutely no intention of getting married, just to string a woman along longer.

The loser is great at promises, but he sucks at follow-through. When you show anger and frustration, he makes more promises, but these are promises he has no intention of keeping. He's just too lazy to look for someone new. It's easier to keep promising you the moon than it is to find another woman who will play his games.

You only hear from him when he's had a bad day.
The selfishness of a loser puts him in a place where he could care less about your bad day, but if he's having a bad day, he wants your full attention. You may begin to notice that the only time you hear from him is when he's frustrated, depressed or horny.

A great guy doesn't want you around solely to comfort him or have sex with him. He's in it to be there for you and to build something with you, not to dump on you and use you when it's convenient.

He uses your money.
A loser is quite comfortable letting you bring home the bacon. If he loses his job and needs your help for a few weeks, that's one thing, but if this behavior goes on for more than a few weeks, you've snagged a loser.

Quality men find having a job and being able to support their loved ones very important to them. Asking a woman to help financially is a very uncomfortable position to be in and, if he asks at all, it won't be for long. The status of a good job means everything to a great guy because he wants to be honorable and he has integrity.

Your status is his status.
The more status you have, the more likely this guy is to try and use it to his advantage. If you have a great job, he'll be proud of it—but not proud of you, just proud he snagged you. He'll show off your nice car and home as if they're his own. This guy wants you around for that status.

Your status can simply be knowing people he considers to be the right people or being famous. There is something about you that he wishes he had, but since he doesn't, he'll be quite content to use what you've earned.

He's always the victim of the story.
Nothing is ever the fault of the loser, from his reasons for being late or not showing up at all to why he's out of money and needs yours and everything in between. This type of person accepts responsibility for absolutely nothing in his life. Everything happens to him.

He complains constantly about his boss, his job, his coworkers and anything else that's on his mind now. It isn't his fault he didn't get the promotion. Surely, he deserved it, you know—because he works so hard and all.

Exposing the Loser

Exposing the loser isn't hard. It goes back to the boundary discussion we've had before. Boundaries put a quick end to a relationship with a loser. He goes MIA, that's breaking a boundary for how you expect to be treated. End of relationship.

Grow your confidence.
When you are a confident woman, you don't need to settle for a loser. He is **not** the only guy willing to pay attention to you. Confident, quality men will line up to date a confident woman.

Being confident means you're engaged in life, not waiting for life to happen to you. It means you:

- Are pursuing those hobbies and passions, keeping yourself too busy to worry about that loser you just dumped
- Have a busy social life with friends and family, getting out there and meeting new people and enjoying your relationships with those who are special to you
- Have built the story of your life and it's an intriguing story to tell, men want to hear it
- Are interesting because of everything I just listed
- Have put dating on pause to lift your confidence and self-esteem so you don't fall into the trap losers and users set for you

- Can expose any loser or user for what he is, now that your eyes have been wiped clean of those rose-colored glasses
- Have set boundaries, based on your own values and beliefs and you honor yourself by sticking to those boundaries, no matter how handsome the guy standing in front of you is

Do your research.
With social media today, there is no good reason to skip doing at least a little bit of digging into a potential new suitor. Stalk a new guy a little. What type of posts does he put out there for the world to see? Is he always complaining or dumping on people? Does he look like he might share some of your passions? Check him out and see if you share any friends that you can ask about him.

While you've been advised to date with your head and not your heart already in this chapter, it's worth repeating. Don't allow your heart to get involved too soon. You won't give your research the credit it deserves.

Slow down the dating process.
Don't allow that biological clock ticking stuff to blind you to what an idiot a guy might be. Think of it like getting that speeding ticket. By the time the officer stopped you, called in your info, wrote up your ticket and got you on your way again, you could have been where you were going—even *if* you were going the speed limit. Which one really saved you time?

Dating is the same way. If you're in a big rush, you don't see what's really going on. You're already buying bride magazines and studying The Knot to learn the newest trends in weddings, two weeks into the relationship.

I've said it before, and I'll say it again. Date for fun. Go do fun things. Have adventures together. Get to know one another. Put him through some of those tests and see how he comes out. Once you've allowed yourself to get to know him, and you determine that he's a good guy, then you can let your heart get into it, maybe just a little.

Don't loosen your boundaries.
Men tend to get ahead of themselves in relationships. Their mouths sort of cut loose with things their mind has no intention of following through on. For example, three weeks into a relationship, he offers you a drawer at his house. You say no.

Why? Because, for one thing, it's way too soon for something like that. Ideally, you haven't even slept with him yet because your boundaries don't allow that. All this is, at this stage of the relationship, is him trying to play on your emotions. He's too lazy to go out and find another girlfriend, so if he keeps wooing you with what he thinks you want, he doesn't need to go back to hunting for someone new to suck the life out of.

Four Test Dates to Weed Out Users and Losers

While I've given you tactics on how to expose the loser and user, here are four very good methods of weeding both out.

The Meet His Friends Date

Suggest that you all get together, you, him and his friends. You could meet at a pub or you could have a backyard barbeque. Maybe you gather to watch football or something else.

We draw people close to us who are most like us, so his friends will be a tell-tale sign of what type of guy he really is. If they seem warm and welcoming, kind and respectful, you probably have nothing to worry about.

If, on the other hand, they're jerks, chances are so is your guy.

If his friends do seem to be good guys, where does he fit in? Is he different when he's around them? Does he set you aside to hang with them, or does he make sure you're entertained as well? He should be proud to show you off to his friends.

The Meet Your Friends Date

Your friends have your back and they will not be quiet about any guy they feel is using you or bad for you in any way. Let your friends take a crack at him. Let them ask him the questions you're too afraid to ask and let them come up with their own questions.

Your besties will be sure to tell you if he checks out other women when you dip into the restroom, or if he hits on one of them when you step away.

The Too Much to Drink Date

Alcohol is like truth serum to a man. Most men will be more honest with you when they're loaded. Of course, the trick here is for you to stay sober. You can do this a couple of ways—either accompany him someplace and let him go to town while you nurse the same drink all night or drop in on him and his friends after you suspect he's had a few too many.

How does he behave when he's had a few? Is he rude, loud, obnoxious? Does he start fights or become loud and antagonistic? His behavior while he's out will tell you anything you need to know about him. I had close friend in high school who slept in dumpsters after drinking!

The Meet His Family Date

This is a date that's more likely to happen after you've dated for a while, so don't rely on this one as an early signal. Many men won't take a woman to meet his family unless they're really interested, so don't be put off if he won't take you for a while.

Once you do get to meet his family, though, pay attention! These people know him better than anyone else. They've seen his best and worst sides.

Watch how he treats his mother. This tells you a lot about what type of man he is. If he doesn't respect her, he is unlikely to respect any woman in his life. The flip side of that, of course, is that he's a momma's boy. This can be okay in small doses, but too much of it can be a different red flag.

The Snoozers

There is hope for the snoozer. This guy can be converted into a Mr. Right with time and patience, but how do you know if you've got a snoozer on your hands? A snoozer could be actively dating, but what he really wants is to settle down.

This type of guy isn't a pushover. He wants to win and succeed like any other confident man, but he might need to be teased along and trained first. He's like a diamond in the rough.

You will need to stick to your boundaries with this guy, and help him understand, gently, what those boundaries are. Make sure you're challenging him and keep intriguing him with interesting bits of your story from time to time.

Never, ever feed a guy your whole story at once. I don't care how wonderful he is, he doesn't want to hear it in one sitting. He wants to peel back the layers and discover it slowly.

This type of guy has worked hard, and he has earned his way in his career. Be sure to make him work hard to earn you in his life as well!

The Snoozer's Patterns of Behavior

He is frustratingly inconsistent.
Some days, he's your knight in shining armor and other days, he's completely flubbing the whole thing. Where there are no real glimpses of hope with a loser or user, there

are some with a snoozer. When a user or loser shows you some sign of him being a great guy, it's for his own gain, not yours. A snoozer will come through for you.

You need to spell out your expectations.
A snoozer might not be towing the line in your relationship. What that means will depend on how long you've been together. You essentially need to train this guy on how to treat you. You need to set those boundaries and teach him how to stick to them. If you're living together, discuss with him a division of labor that works for both of you.

This type of guy is willing to learn, but he's often clueless as to where to start. This is good for you because you can train him to be what you want him to be. A snoozer will come around. A user will be offended and will not comply.

His baggage is light.
Ultimately, this is a good guy and his past probably isn't too bad, so he's not bringing a ton of negative baggage into your relationship. The odds are that there are one or two small things in his past that you can help him identify while being supportive and all will be well.

Notice I didn't say that you fix them for him, you help him. You can't fix any man.

How to Convert a Snoozer into Mr. Right

Show him how to be Mr. Right.
If you're able to help him identify an issue that needs to be fixed, be supportive of him and help him see the solution. Let him fix it for himself knowing that his award will be you. This is important to him and key in his pathway to being Mr. Right.

Don't make him your hobby.
By nature, most women are nurturers. It's why you get to be the Mommies. Unfortunately, too many women carry this into their relationships and they over-nurture a man.

Even though you've found a great guy, it's important for you to maintain your own hobbies, passions and friendships. You should not give any of those up for a man. It's too smothering for him and it's unhealthy for you.

Don't support bad behavior.
When he has done something wrong, retreat to your social life. You don't need to say a thing, just spend an evening with your girlfriends and let him sort it out. You leaving, especially if you do it in a non-threatening way, does cause him to worry that you might leave him. If he's any sort of a good guy, this will stir a little competitiveness in him, and he'll straighten himself right up.

This type of behavior from you nudges him back into chasing you again, and men love the chase. Remind him that you're worth chasing by escaping, now and then, to hang with friends, play around with your hobbies or get engrossed in your passion.

Reward his good behavior.
When he does something great, be sure to let him know about it. "Gee Gregg, thanks for mowing the lawn for me. What a surprise when I returned from work! Thank you!"

Maintain radio silence during the time apart.
Instead of texting him all day, save some stuff for when you're together. This gives you something interesting to talk about when you get together next time. Of course, I don't want you to be completely silent, but don't share every blessed thing that happens in your day with him. He doesn't need you checking in, every hour, to ask him how his day is going.

Break from usual.
Routine is boring. Change your hairstyle, color or cut. Take a Camaro for a test drive and tell him about it. Bring home two kitties from the shelter. Show up wearing something completely different from your normal date night attire. Change things up to keep him on his toes.

Don't let him get to the point where he knows exactly where you'll be at any given moment. Let him wonder what you'll do next that will intrigue him. He'll love it.

If you find yourself in a bit of a disagreement, retreat first. Usually a man will walk out of the situation first while the woman trails behind, either begging him not to go or screaming obscenities at him. Instead, you walk away first. Head to your chick retreat or go out with your friends.

This is called Man Mode—Learn more about it by going to www.whoholdsthecardsnow.com/man-mode-infographic-2.

If his normal way of dealing with something is to go sit in the living room and turn on the television, you go to your office or bedroom and turn on the music. Whatever he would do—you do it first—your way.

This does two things. It helps him sort through whatever was going on, and it also causes him to think, "hmmm" because you just acted like a guy and he recognizes that behavior—although not from you. He knows how to deal with it because it's familiar.

Standing there screaming at him won't win you a thing and he won't respond. Walk away and see what happens.

Speak his language.
Suppose your guy is spending a lot of time with his friends and it's starting to get on your last nerve. Fine. Rather than getting all upset about it, slamming doors and initiating a yelling match, go get dressed up and hang out with your friends. Make sure he sees you leave, looking hot, and trot yourself out the door with few words, "Okay Gregg, I'm going out with Steph and Jen for a while. See you later!"

Huh?

He understands this behavior because it's what he would do. Looking hot when you walk out the door is the icing on the cake. He's now wondering if any guys are hitting on you. He's wondering if you've found someone who won't hang out with his friends all the time. He's thinking he needs to change!

Mr. Right

When you find a great guy, he won't look anything like these guys—well maybe a little like the snoozer, but otherwise, you won't find any of those patterns of behavior in him.

If you did the exercises in your workbook, you've identified who Mr. Right is for you and all the qualities you desire in your great guy.

Of course, no man, or woman is perfect, but if a guy is perfect for you, you're all set!

Meeting Men Where They Are

Where you will find the man of your dreams will depend on several factors, not the least of which is age. If you're young, you may like hanging out with your friends in bars or pubs. These can be great locations to meet men, but they can also be shark tanks.

For older folks, the bar scene might not be your first choice. I still enjoy them, but I go into them determined to help women like you, and I have fun doing it.

Meeting guys comes back to what your interests are. You learned this earlier. If you like sports, go to sports venues. If you're into diving, join diving groups. If you're into RV'ing, join RV clubs.

For example, I just bought an RV. I've always had a passion for traveling and living in an RV. I'm not sure why, but I thought, "What the heck?". My friends don't RV, and frankly think I'm crazy, but I don't care. I want to go RV'ing. So, what did I do? I joined an RV club where I'm meeting fellow RV'ers.

Now, I am meeting people who are interested in RV'ing and can join me on the road to Yellowstone or wherever we feel like going!

If you're into wine, go to wine tastings. If you believe in giving to charity, go to charity events. Do you love animals? Volunteer at your local animal shelter. Do you see my point? You don't have to go find your guy directly. Instead, let your guy find you while you pursue an interest you enjoy or think you might enjoy. This takes all the pressure off meeting a man.

It's this pressure that leads to frustration. Once you feel frustrated, you start making bad choices. Bad choices lead to dating the first guy who shows interest instead of carefully choosing a guy who's right for you. After that date, you just give up and decide to stay single. Break the cycle by pursuing venues of interest instead of random bars.

In your workbook, you did an exercise where you wrote down positive and negative qualities of the men from your past. In that exercise, you probably uncovered clues as to where your guy might be hanging out.

This would be a great time to complete Exercise 13!

Now that you know where your ideal man might be hanging out, let's look at a few possibilities and examine how you can own each different scenario.

Owning the Bar Scene

Not everyone is comfortable hanging out in a bar and if this is a new venue to you, you might feel more than a little bit anxious at the thought.

Don't let that dissuade you. Keep reading. I will help you become more comfortable with it. While this section is about the bar scene, this works at any venue of your choosing.

No location is full of *only* great guys. Whether you're in a bar or a high-class charity event, there will be sharks. Fortunately for you, you have the previous chapter to help you decipher which guys are the good guys and which ones are looking to get into your pants.

My goal in this chapter is to help you understand what men are thinking when they see you in a bar. I will preface this information by saying that I make no excuses for my gender.

You're Already New and Improved—Show it!

In the short time since you began reading this book, you've already changed, a lot. This is good! It might not feel comfortable yet. It might feel like I'm pushing you too hard, but I assure you, you're ready to show off what you have!

The truth is that the journey you're on will take time. You're in a growth phase, and part of that growth involves exploring. It's through exploration that you will continue to grow. It's all well and good to sit here, read and do the exercises, but it's not practical experience.

When people go to college for many professions, part of their learning is through practical experience or internships. Doctors, nurses, artists, designers and workers in all sorts of trades go out into the field to put their hands into what they're learning.

That's what you're about to do too! It's time to start your dating internship. You're entering a new learning phase of your life and it's an exciting time. It might feel a little scary at times but staring down that fear and overcoming it will be a huge step in building your confidence and self-esteem!

Dress for success.
First, dress in what feels comfortable for who you are, not what you think a guy will like. Second, dress in a way that shows off your best features but isn't too revealing. Frumpy, baggy clothing isn't nearly as attractive on anyone, male or female, as clothing that fits well and hugs the curves in important places.

Think about the last guy you swooned over. I bet he was wearing a t-shirt that hugged his muscular upper body and jeans that fit just right.

Men don't need to see the whole show. In fact, this takes away the mystery for them. A great guy would rather use his imagination to envision what you look like, underneath that sexy white blouse or the beautiful red sweater you're wearing.

Choose approachable over high maintenance.
If you're looking to be someone's toy, fine. Wear all the high-end stuff you want. Those guys recognize it, but most men wouldn't know a Coach purse from one you got at Walmart. On the rare occasion they do recognize your high-end accessories, they might be turned off.

No man wants to think you're dating him for his money first, unless he's looking for arm candy. Men are very protective of their money because it's how they plan to support you some day. It's their measure of how well they can take care of you.

Now, don't go getting all feminist on me. I know you can support yourself, and trust me, a great man values this about you, but he needs to know that if push comes to shove, he can support his family.

Look confident.
Confidence levels the playing field for all women. When a man scans a room, he's looking for a woman who isn't hiding behind her hair or sunglasses. He's looking for a woman who doesn't think she needs to use sex appeal to win him over. He's looking for a woman who seems to be enjoying

herself, shows open body language and isn't huddled up in a closed circle of friends.

Remember, I've told you a few times now that the shy guy might be the one you want to date, but if he sees you closed up in a huddle with your friends, he's not going to approach. It's one thing for a girl to shoot you down. It's a whole other thing to get shot down in front of a group of attractive women.

Remember to leave an open spot next to you as an open invitation for that shy guy to approach. He will approach if the environment feels safe.

Make eye contact.
If you see a man you're interested in, make eye contact but then, look away. Give it a minute or so and then look his way again. Don't stare. Look his way and then look away. It's a very powerful way to send a message.

While you're making eye contact, be sure to smile and don't forget the **red lipstick**. As it turns out, science tells us that men are attracted to red lipstick. Who knew?

Initiate casual contact.
On your way to the restroom, walk past the jukebox or the pool table and deliver a casual touch on your way by. It doesn't have to be anything formal. Just make light contact as you pass.

This is a subtle signal, but one that tells him that if he approaches you, he probably won't get shut down—at least not right away.

Change your 'spots'.
I love this one and I discovered it quite by accident. Men put labels on women. Use it to your advantage!

Suppose you show up at a bar right after work. You've still got your hair done up in a more formal do, you might even still be wearing something more formal. Let it ride for a while, then let your hair down or take off a jacket or sweater. This is particularly effective if the change is dramatic. Maybe you're all dressed up from work, but you slide off the sweater you have on over your top and a tattoo is revealed.

A man who probably had you labeled as being out of his league is suddenly quite intrigued. The change in appearance breaks the label he had created for you. Women do this too—it's not a man only thing. We place labels on people we don't know. We might label the "Mean old lady at the grocery store" because she was grimacing the whole time. Maybe she just found out her cat died.

By changing your 'spots' you break the label he placed on you. He becomes fixated on what you will do next. Mystery is created!

Unleashing Your Inner Tigress at a High-End Event

You may discover that your type of guy is more likely to be found at a wine-tasting or a charity event. Great! Let's go get him!

In this instance, you'll need to dress accordingly. Go for sexy, but not slutty.

Sexy comes from your confidence and is usually seen on a woman who is dressed in a classy way. Her hair and makeup are appropriate for the venue. She is wearing clothing that is suitable for the type of event she's attending, and she is comfortable in that clothing.

A sexy woman is a woman who knows she has more than sex appeal going for her. She's intelligent, confident and she knows who she is and where she's headed.

It might be scary to attend an event like this by yourself, so ask a friend to go with you. The trick is to arrive 30 minutes before she does and give yourself time to own this venue without being attached to someone else. At first, this will be scary, but if you do it enough times, it won't be. You may even find yourself comfortable attending by yourself. That's a big win!

Also, men will 'label' you as single walking in which will create quite a stir.

If you are hunting in these waters, it shouldn't feel uncomfortable to you. Generally speaking, people don't tend to 'date down' too far. If we rank people on a scale from one to ten, a five won't date beyond a three or a seven. So, if you really don't think you're cut out for this type of event, work up to it.

I consider myself a six—Shakira won't date me…damn!

Attend events that aren't quite so high-end and get comfortable there. Just like anything else, build up to feeling comfortable in new environments.

Remember, this is a journey and you're still at the beginning.

Sporting Events

Some women truly enjoy sports, more so than some men do. If you're into sports and your ideal guy is also, you might find him at a sporting event.

Now, let's define sporting event for our purposes. Your mind probably went to a pro football, basketball, hockey or baseball game, but it doesn't need to be that type of event.

If you enjoy bowling, join a co-ed league. If you love soccer, play in a co-ed league or hang out before or after your games when men might be milling around.

Of course, you'll want to dress appropriately for these events, again, avoiding the too-sexy attire.

Unleashing Your Inner Tigress

The time has come to put what you've started learning into action. You just learned how to use specific venues to your advantage. Now, it's time to learn some general rules of being a tigress.

What is a tigress?

Your inner tigress is the confident, happy woman you are becoming. You are fearless when it comes to getting what you want. You're driven and passionate. You're writing the story of your life with each new friendship you build, hobby you engage in, passion you pursue.

Your inner tigress is still evolving and will continue to evolve throughout the remainder of your life, if you allow her to do so. She is the you who dates great men and chooses the one who is best for her. She is the you who follows her dreams, sets goals and pursues them with drive and dedication.

This Tigress attracts men!

Your Inner Tigress is Sexy

Sexy isn't the same as slutty. You've learned that by now, but what does it mean to be sexy?

Ambition

A sexy tigress is ambitious. She knows what she wants, and she goes after it until she gets where she wants to be. This doesn't mean she hurts others or steps on other people's toes to get where she wants to be.

Ambition is sexy because it gives a man a clear picture of your own goals and how they might align with his. This helps him define his own drive and purpose. He understands that, with you, he can do anything. Together, you are unstoppable.

Confidence

Confidence is not the same as perfection. Hopefully you've learned that by now in this book. Nobody is perfect. You just need to find someone who is perfect for you and for whom you are perfect.

A confident woman can be spotted from a distance because it shows in her walk, how she carries herself, whether she makes eye contact or not and her smile that lights up the room.

Men find confidence sexy because they know they're dealing with a woman who isn't afraid to go after what she wants, and he hopes one of the things you want is him!

Passion

Passion is an awesome quality to see in someone. A passionate person almost has a fire in their eyes when they're talking about that thing that has become so important to them.

When I do video summits, my passion and energy for helping women shines through. People are drawn to this because they recognize my genuine desire to help them.

Men love to see you doing something that you just love so much you almost can't put it into words. It's almost contagious and it adds mystery and intrigue, which men love.

Honesty

While being truthful is important, this type of honesty relates more to being your own self—that uniqueness you uncovered early in the workbook.

Men love to find women who aren't afraid to be themselves, instead of mindlessly forging ahead with the flock. Honesty also gives him assurance that he can build a trusting relationship with you.

Class

Class isn't about expensive handbags or shoes. Class is about how much dignity you possess. Classy people respect others and treat others with kindness and sincerity. Class is about your attitude toward life and those who are living it alongside you.

When you're classy, you have a positive, upbeat attitude that draws others in. People are naturally drawn to your positivity and your kindness lets them know it's okay to approach.

Intelligence

Intelligence isn't about how far you went in college or where you grew up. Intelligence is built partly from personal growth and a desire to learn.

When a man is dating a woman, he wants to be able to have engaging conversations and perhaps even a debate or two. This doesn't mean you need to know everything about everything, but it does mean you have opinions about what you do know and you're not afraid to share them in a healthy conversation.

These opinions and conversations are derived from all your interests, passions and adventures—not from your college education level.

Men find this sexy because an engaging conversation can be intriguing and challenging. If you challenge him on whether the Patriots are the best team in the NFL, you'd better be prepared to back it up, and when you do, he'll be blown away.

If you challenge him on politics, be prepared to back up your opinion.

This doesn't mean you set yourself up for arguments, but you're prepared to provide your opinion and listen to his. You can agree to disagree, or you can find common ground and find something you both enjoy.

Self-Respect and Self-Worth

A sexy woman respects herself and takes good care of herself. She practices good hygiene and lives a relatively healthy lifestyle. This type of woman invests in herself and is always making the best choices for herself.

She eats healthy, works out and recognizes that taking care of herself means she can be there for her loved ones.

Men find this sexy because it helps them see that you value life, yourself and know how to be healthy. If this is important for him, it's one more assurance that he's on the right path dating you.

Respect for Others

A sexy woman doesn't gossip or say mean things about other people, whether she knows them or not. She treats everyone with respect and is gracious. Her respect for others extends to animals and children. This also means she doesn't engage in jealousy or other behaviors that have a negative result.

She sees beyond someone's looks to their inner beauty. Men find this sexy and love that you're not into drama. No man wants to get in the middle of some sort of drama. We like to stay drama-free.

Open to New Experiences
It's great to have your own interests, hobbies and passions, but it's also really attractive when a guy can say, "Would you like to go fishing this Saturday morning?" and she says, "Well, I've never been fishing before but I'd love to give it a try!"

As a couple, you will grow and develop new interests together and this helps him understand that you'll be open to trying things he finds interesting. He will likely reciprocate and try something you're interested in.

Your Inner Tigress Knows how to Make Him Feel Special

In the same way you like a man to make you feel special, he likes to feel special too, although probably not in the same way.

Laugh at His Jokes
I know. He tells corny jokes. We all do it because it helps lighten the mood. The thing is that if you don't laugh at his jokes, he'll feel really let down.

Rather than sit there like a brick wall, laugh at it, even if it's a dumb joke. It'll stroke his ego a little and he might need that. If he really likes you, he may be a little nervous and this is his way of breaking the ice.

Mirror Him

Mirroring is a great technique to use because it makes the two of you feel as if you're synchronized. If you've just met a new guy and you really like him, subtly mirror his actions. If he crosses one leg over the other, wait a few moments and then do the same. If he touches his hair, wait a few minutes then touch your hair.

This is sometimes an activity couples do unconsciously, after they've been together for a while.

Give Him a Compliment

This needs to be a genuine compliment, not just something you say to be nice, "Boy Jim, it was really great how you helped that elderly couple walk across the icy parking lot." He likes to know that he's done something you appreciate.

Look Your Best

Men like to show off what they have. Now, don't get your dander up—I'm not calling you a possession, but he does take pride in having you by his side.

Therefore, he will really appreciate it if you look your best when you're out together, especially if it's with his friends.

He wants to show you off. He's proud of his relationship with you.

Learn His Love Language

Dr. Gary Chapman revealed five love languages that we all speak. Usually, however, there are one or two that we prefer. When you learn his love language, you will be able to make him feel special by showing him in the love language that most speaks to him.

Words of Affirmation

This love language is about telling someone you love them. Like the compliment example above, you use your words to let your guy know when he's done something you like.

Acts of Service

In this love language, your guy will appreciate it when you do things for him, like finding out what his favorite cookie recipe is from his mom and then baking up a batch!

Receiving Gifts

Some people enjoy receiving your love in a little gift. This doesn't need to be anything elaborate either. It could be a couple of his favorite cookies or a six-pack of his favorite football watching beverage.

Quality Time

There is really no substitute for quality time in a relationship anyway, but if your guy's love language is quality time, then he will appreciate it when you set aside time for the two of you to connect. Even if it's just an hour or so to sit and talk, he'll really love knowing you care.

Physical Touch
If your guy likes physical touch, he will feel your love in the little touches you provide. Maybe it's just a light touch on his arm or a massage after a long day. Regardless, he will enjoy feeling your touch as a show of your love.

Allow Him His Time

Just like you've created your chick retreat, or she shed, your guy needs his time alone as well. If he doesn't have such a space, help him create one and then respect it. If he likes to enjoy a glass of his favorite wine or whiskey, keep it stocked for him.

A man will retreat to this place when he's stressed, bummed or feeling a lot of emotions about something that happened. Before he can talk to you about it, he needs to sort it out. If you respect his need for this time, you'll both be a lot happier.

Do Something for Him While You're Doing Something for Yourself

If you decide to run out for coffee, ask him if he'd like one. If you decide to sneak a brownie mid-afternoon, bring him one. Let him know he's on your mind for even those small things. It makes it extra special if you're going somewhere that relates to something he loves, like a sport or movie, and you bring him something. You could be shopping for soccer cleats for the kids, but you see those sweat-absorbing socks he loves, so you grab him a pair.

It's the Little Things

If you haven't noticed by now, most of the things I've mentioned here are small, but they add up! There are no grand gestures of love here. It's more about letting him know you're thinking about him, you appreciate him, or you want to spend time with him. It's the same things you probably want from him.

Your Inner Tigress Takes Risks

Staring down fear and taking it on is unnerving, but it's something a man will really find attractive. Of course, we need to define risky behavior first, and for the attractiveness factor, riskiness applies more to legal risk-taking as opposed to illegal risk-taking.

In other words, he'll be attracted to a woman who likes to ski, go hiking or climbing, rafting and so on, but he won't be attracted to a woman who loves to shoplift, vandalize mailboxes or drink and drive.

Risk taking has other benefits. When you do these activities as a couple, it's a bonding experience. You're building memories and intimacy and that's a win-win.

Risk taking also helps you continue to build your confidence and self-esteem. The more fear you overcome, the more confident you'll become.

Meet and Attract Him

It's true that men love the chase, but it's also true that a man will be truly flattered if a woman approaches him first. This is a big deal and it's truly unique.

I think women often don't realize that men have fragile egos. Men are thought of as the tough gender—we're tough on the outside and on the inside, but the truth is that we're just as afraid of being shot down as you are, perhaps more so if we're with friends.

Since this is rare behavior from women, it's a very effective way to get a man's attention. Most women won't have the nerve to approach a man. Even if things don't work out, you still made an impression!

The key is not to be too subtle. A man might not figure out what you're attempting to do. While some of the actions you take—a smile, a glance, a light brush across his arm when you pass by—might get his attention, they're not overt enough for him to realize you're truly interested.

Men are accustomed to being rejected by women, so they need stronger signals that you're really into them. You're more likely to be approached if your signals are strong rather than subtle. Don't just sit there and smile, thinking he knows you're interested. Walk up and say hello!

You can use the signals I'm about to describe as your launching off point.

Flirt a Little

If his looks remind you of someone who's notoriously handsome and famous, tell him. This is an immediate ego stroke, which is always a win.

If you've met him before and you notice that he got a haircut or seems to be different in a positive way, make sure to compliment the change.

Be careful not to pour it on too thick. Just let him know you're interested. Let him do the rest.

Make Eye Contact

Make eye contact with a guy by looking straight into his eyes. Don't stare, though, and look away after just a moment or two. Be sure to add a smile for added effect.

After you look away, be sure to look back, again with a smile. This is a definite signal to him that you're interested and it's safe to approach.

Use a Light Touch

If you're chatting with your new friend, brush your hand across his as you reach for a pretzel or nacho. Subtly touch his arm as you stand up to go to the restroom. You can even go as far as lightly stroking his hand while he's telling you one of his corny jokes.

Square Your Shoulders

Use an open body stance, with your shoulders squared and facing him. This is the same body language men inadvertently use to signal to you that you're important.

Ask Questions

While you don't want to put him through the Spanish Inquisition, it's a strong signal that you're interested if you ask him some questions. Let him know you're interested by probing into a few of his likes and dislikes. Take your cues from what's going on around you. If he seems interested in a game on TV, ask which team he likes.

React Positively if He Approaches

If a guy approaches you after you've sent signals, it's not a time to become coy. Let him know he didn't misread your cues by reacting positively and showing him in slightly more overt ways that you're interested. Be a good listener. Ask those questions and use touch to your advantage.

Wave Him Over

If you really want to take a bravery test, wave a guy over. If he's with his friends, this will score you **mega** points! Just don't shoot him down right away because that will have the opposite effect!

Encourage Him to Approach

All the signals you sent him may have him thinking you're interested, but he still might be a little nervous about approaching. There are some ways in which you can make him feel more comfortable:

- Leave a seat or open space next to you so he feels like there's room for him

- Allow there to be something about you he can use to initiate a conversation over—color highlights in your hair, a unique scarf or earrings, a hat—anything unique that he can ask about

- Dress in a way that doesn't intimidate a great, but perhaps shy guy—something too revealing or something too high end might turn him off or scare him

- Stay in essentially the same place; it's okay to go dancing or whatever, but have a place where you're rooted for the evening; sit down or wait in the line

- It's fine to be with a few female friends, but keep your male friends at home if you're out to meet a man; men will immediately believe this guy belongs to you and they won't approach

Be Prepared with an Adjusted Mindset

Now, you know how to snag the guy you're interested in, but do you have a plan of action for what happens next? I know it will be a little nerve wracking to have the guy approach, but if you stutter and drool, it's not going to look so good.

Your goal for this first attraction is to let him know you're interested and perhaps get his phone number. Don't give him yours—just get his.

Now, your intention is no longer to make him your boyfriend, it's just to get his number and let him know for sure that you're interested. All the actions previously listed will help you do both.

It's Okay to Date Multiple Men

I guarantee you that when you first date a guy, he's dating other women as well. This is okay. You're still trying one another on for size. You're not in a committed relationship.

You need to do the same. It's okay for you to date multiple men at once. It doesn't make you sleezy or a bad girl or anything like that. It makes you someone who is weighing your options.

It also places you in a place of abundance, instead of scarcity. When you're only dating one guy, you have no other options. How do you know if you like him or if someone else may be even better for you? Allow yourself to have choices.

In the process of dating multiple men, you also gain experience with dating and you start to fine-tune that list you made—you remember—the one with the traits of your ideal man. Along with the positive experience, you'll probably have one or two guys move on. The sting of this is much less painful if you've got other guys you're interested in.

Conversational Tactics

While a guy can screw up a conversation quickly, for women, it's more difficult to mess up. You don't need some cute pickup line because any time you approach a man, it will be such a unique experience that it won't matter what you say.

Once you initiate conversation, he'll likely take over, whether guided at first by nerves or genuine interest. A shy guy might not jump right into conversation, so you may need to massage the conversation along at first, but as soon as he feels comfortable, he'll start talking more.

If you're anywhere other than a bar, you're probably in a place in which you both share an interest. A charity event or a wine tasting, a cooking class or learning to scuba dive all will have a common interest and conversation flows easily.

Since this is an interest, or maybe even a passion of yours, you should have some sort of opinion and knowledge about the topic. If it's a wine tasting, you probably know a little something about wine and can strike up an intelligent conversation about the wines you're sampling.

This type of conversation presents a man with a challenge, especially if you inject a little playfulness into it. This piques his interest in you and he becomes more engaged. From here, you can start to form a connection and attraction will start to grow.

Keep it Balanced

While you're conversing, keep the conversation balanced. Don't constantly be the one talking. If you find yourself in this position, stop and say something like, "Gee, I've been going on and on. What do you think about..." Shift the conversation back into his court and be sure to keep it balanced.

Also, try to avoid being argumentative or combative. You're trying to win him over and arguing with him won't do it. If you disagree, that's fine, but do so in a respectful and even a playful way. If you two end up together, this won't be your last disagreement. Show him right off that you can handle it.

Take Charge—Temporarily

A quality man likes to be in control, but he's willing to give that up for a little while, especially when he's still getting to know you. You don't need to do much, and you don't want to do this often, but don't be afraid to take him by the hand and say something like, "Come on Jon, let's get our drinks refreshed" or "I wanted to take a look at this painting over here. Care to join me?" or even, "This is the Packer's game, but I'd really like to see what the Colts are doing. Let's go over here and watch for a while."

This is attractive to a man for a few reasons:

- You surprised him by taking charge, if only for a moment
- You exhibited confidence; you showed him you know what you want and you're not afraid to go after it

- You injected a little mystery; you have him wondering what you'll have him getting into next

Once you've taken charge, allow him to retake control. A while later, go ahead and take control for a little while again. You're showing him that you aren't intimidated by the situation and you are a take-charge kind of woman, but you're also willing to allow him to play his role. As with anything else, balance your moments of control with more moments where you allow him to have the control.

You Have the Tools Now

You've got just about all the tools you need to attract the guy you've had your eye on now. It's up to you to muster up the courage to try it for the first time. You are no longer asking why you can't find a great guy because you've identified what a great guy looks like to you and you know how to attract and intrigue him.

Your confidence is growing as you complete the exercises in your workbook and start taking your new skills for a test drive. You're developing hobbies, initiating boundaries, setting goals and working on loving yourself. All of this helps you develop into the confident woman a confident man will be attracted to.

You have the advantage over most of the women in the room, regardless of where you are, because you've learned a few secret weapons from a man!

It's Time to Meet Men on Your Terms

During an average week, how many men do you come across who could potentially be *the one*? Probably very few, right? The grocery store clerk and the UPS guy aren't in the running unless they've really got something you like. There might be a guy or two in the coffee shop or when you stop for lunch, but do you initiate any conversation? Probably not.

It's time to learn some great methods for meeting men. Are you ready?

Attend a Local Single's Event
Whether you decide to go as a volunteer or you go to meet new people, a single's event is a great place to meet men because you're all there for that same purpose. Many groups

today are even specialized. Singles who ski or single bowling leagues. There are singles groups for just about anything these days and Meetup.com is a great place to find them.

Go to a Sports Bar

Sports bars can be intimidating for women because the male to female ratio is out of balance. There are way more men there than women, but this is good for you because it means you've got your pick of the pack!

Okay, so you hate sports. That's fine. You don't need to know much about sports to go to a sports bar and meet great men. I know I told you to be able to converse, so have some idea who's playing, what sports season it is and maybe choose a favorite team. If you can't come up with one, use your dad's favorite or the favorite team of someone you know. Take a crash course and head on in!

Men like teaching women things; it makes them feel worthy and knowledgeable. Go in and ask a few questions. You'll meet some great guys and you might even discover you like basketball, or football, or baseball, or whatever.

Get in Line

If the man of your dreams is in line for a beer at the hockey game, get in line behind him. Be interested in whatever he seems fixed on. If it's the halftime show, comment on it. If he's studying the menu board, say something like, "I know. I can't decide between popcorn and nachos. What do you think?"

If you see your dream guy getting into the elevator, hop in. Who cares if it takes you three floors out of your way? You might find Mr. Right!

Love Your Single Status

So many times, women feel like they're 'less than' if they're not dating someone. Their friends and family are always asking when they'll get back out there.

Enjoy this time while you're single. If you're truly on the hunt for the man you'll spend the rest of your life with, then this is the time to live it up!

Have fun dating. That's what men are doing. Don't worry about racking up those milestones. Just because he holds your hand or kisses you on the cheek, it doesn't mean anything. It just means he felt like holding your hand or kissing you on the cheek.

Dating is about getting to know someone, not picking out china patterns. This is a time to learn more about the men you date and get to know yourself a little better too.

The type of man you identified as ideal may need a little tweaking, but you won't figure this out unless you take a few different men on.

Examining Why You've Dated the Wrong Type of Guy in the Past

Lack of Confidence

A big part of the reason why you've dated the wrong type of guy in the past is because your confidence was lower, and you weren't making good choices.

Many women who have low confidence date from a position of desperation. This makes you more likely to be thankful some guy choses you than it does to put you in the position of weeding out the losers.

Not Knowing What You Really Want

You went through the exercise about men for one reason—to avoid this trap. Most people continue to go after the same type of person, not because they are particularly fond of that type of person, but because it's comfortable and it's a known entity.

Always going after a biker type feels safe and comfortable, but when you did your assessment, was that still the type of guy you identified in the exercises?

It's important to examine the positive and negative traits of the men from your past and use that information to determine the right guy for you.

Likes attract Likes

Low confidence people gravitate toward one another. That's why, if your confidence was low in the past, you attracted the losers and users. They're low confidence also.

As you build your confidence, you may notice that your circle of female friends changes for the same reason. You no longer can tolerate the backbiting and negativity. Your circle has grown wider and you've found new friends who share your interests.

As you grow, you desire and attract high confidence men. That's just how it works. It begins when you realize that you need to grow before you bring a man into your life—most people have this backwards.

You Went for the Hot Guy Instead of the Right Guy

It's fine to go after the attractive guy, but this can lead you into a position of wearing blinders. The hot guy might be throwing up red flags that he's a user, but you're mesmerized by his smoking hot good looks and you miss the signs.

Keep your eyes wide open when you date. Think of the first few dates as meetings instead of dates. You're meeting a great new guy so you can do something fun together. After he's passed a few tests, you can consider it a date. Meanwhile, Mr. Hottie may or may not have made it into the pool of men you choose from.

You Didn't Take the Time to Truly Get to Know One Another

Too often, people start dating and they get too serious too fast. Three months into things, they're living together and talking marriage.

Sure, sometimes this works out, but the truth is that three months probably amounts to very few dates, relatively speaking. In twelve dates, you've just started to peel back the second or third onion layer. You may or may not have met his family yet, but you've probably met his friends.

Take time to get to know one another. Watch how holidays and special occasions are handled. I have a friend, Dave, who has been dating this girl for about nine months. The holidays are approaching, and I can already see him starting to cringe at the long list of events she expects him to attend.

You both must watch and learn during this dating period. Do his opinions of things line up with yours or do you find yourself on opposite sides of the fence?

Slow your roll and really take the time to figure these things out. Things may seem all warm and fuzzy to start, but once the gloves come off and the relationship reaches a new level, changes might start to happen. It's better to find out while you're dating that he hates dogs and you've got three.

You Share Similar Baggage

Common ground is often a reason people get together, but some common ground is detrimental. A great example is two people who like to drink or do drugs.

Another item of baggage people might share is a recent bad breakup. You both end up commiserating over the bad relationship, complaining about your exes.

This might be common ground, but it isn't the right kind of common ground. You want to share positives like interests in specific activities or religion, not alcoholism.

Bad baggage leads to codependent relationships and those are never good.

You Don't Understand Where Happiness Comes From

You learned about happiness earlier, so I won't belabor the point now. You may have believed that your happiness was tied to having a man in your life. Now you know better, and you won't be as likely to make a hasty decision about dating someone new, whether he's the right guy or not.

You Were Tired of Being the Single One

Let's face it, it's no fun when all your friends are dating someone and you're not. You get invited to the parties and either your friends fix you up without you knowing ahead of time, or you go alone and find yourself feeling lonely and maybe even a little embarrassed.

This is that position of desperation you read about before. You might leave an event like that feeling as if you just must find a guy. You're not going to go through that again!

You Initiated a Relationship on Faulty Reasoning

I always cringe when I get an email that starts with, "We were meant to be together" because I know what's coming. They don't understand why they're not together now, but the truth is that *there isn't any meant to be together thing*.

You might meet a guy who seems to be great and you get that same feeling, but until you've gotten to know him better, you just can't be sure. There are many wolves in sheep's clothing. Now, you're smart enough to detect those wolves and toss them to the curb, but in the past, you might not have seen his true fur color.

You Ignored Many Red Flags

I understand a guy who is just out of college living with his parents, but I also know that a quality guy like this is striving to get the job he wants so he can move out on his own.

A man who is 35 and still living at home throws up many major red flags. Again, if he's just found himself in a difficult situation, like a recent divorce, where finances are undecided, okay, but he should be working hard to get his own place.

Another red flag that is completely unacceptable is when a guy abuses you, physically or emotionally. The low self-esteem version of you might have believed it when he said you had it coming, but there is **never** a reason to abuse someone. Still, he brainwashed you into believing it wouldn't happen again, and because you were afraid, you'd never again meet a great guy, you believed him.

The guy who drinks too much throws up many red flags as well. Having one too many every now and then is fine but having one too many every night after work is not. Still, it might be justified by him, you or both, that he's experiencing difficulties and the alcohol makes him feel better, or some sort of twisted logic like that. This type of drinking isn't occasional. It's habitual and it's a red flag.

You Thought You Could Fix Him

I'm sorry to tell you this, but fixing is the responsibility of the person who needs fixing. You cannot fix someone and nobody else can fix you. I can write this book for you, but if you don't do the work, nothing good will come of it. You need to fix you.

Still, you've probably fallen for some cute guy whose flaws were seemingly unremarkable, but once you got into it, you realized they were much greater. You can't make him quit hitting you. You can't make him stop drinking or doing drugs. You can't make him stop working 80 hours a week. You can't heal his emotional wounds. He must do all those things for himself.

The Best First Date

You might think a great first date is dinner or drinks. It's so common it's cliché. Science has proven us wrong, yet again on this one. While dinner is a nice way to sit and talk and enjoy one another's company, if you're trying to stir feelings of love from a man, it's not going to get you anywhere.

Heighten the Emotion

In one study, researchers took men to a scenic area where there were two bridges to walk across. One bridge was sturdy and the other swayed like crazy when you walked across it. At the end of each bridge, a female research assistant presented the men with the task of writing a brief story about their experience. After the men turned in their story, the research assistants gave the men their phone numbers and casually mentioned that the man could call if he wanted to *further discuss his experience.*

The men who went across the solid bridge wrote more 'bland' stories while the men who had walked across the swaying bridge wrote the sexiest stories. The men who had walked across the swaying bridge were also more likely to call the female assistants to *further discuss their experiences.*

Now, having said that, you don't need to go bungee jumping on a first date to get him to fall in love with you, although that's certainly an option. I would suggest something a little tamer like horseback riding, surfing, kayaking or even a walk after a snow when things are quiet and it's a more emotional experience. If you aren't into action, it's perfectly acceptable to go for something emotionally exhausting like a scary movie, a concert by his favorite band, a ballet (if you can get him to go) or even a moving play. If you can find out what tweaks his buttons, you can suggest something like that. Maybe he's into classical music—you can suggest an outing to a classical music event or to the opera. Think in terms of what will get his emotions up or what will make him feel a tad anxious.

In another study, some males were told they would be getting an electric shock that would hurt a bit while others were told it would barely be noticeable. They were then introduced to a female researcher they thought was also going to participate in the experiment. Subsequently, they were asked to fill out a questionnaire about the woman. Those who thought they were going to experience pain rated the female more favorably than those who were told the pain would be minimal, if any.

What is happening here is that, once again, you are stimulating those fight or flight hormones, the PEA, in his brain. This is the same thing we talked about with the eye gaze in the beginning. You're just transferring this from a first meeting to a first date.

Know Your Town
It's difficult to suggest a fun date or one which will heighten the emotion if you don't know much about your town. Whether you're in a small town or a big city, you need to know what's available. Where are the closest bowling alleys? Where can you go for a great hike, to go kayaking or to enjoy a great band? What sports teams are in your town? Where can you go for the best burger, Italian or Greek food? Start checking out these places so you can honestly say, "There's a great burger joint just around the corner from All Star Bowling".

We're Really the Same
While women are verbal, men are action oriented. This shows up in love in all kinds of ways. Men will do things to show they're in love while women will say the words, *I love you*. Women often get frustrated when a man won't say *I love you* and they miss the cues that he truly is in love. Let's transfer this to a first date.

I just suggested to you that you offer up an adventurous or emotionally stirring experience with your man. You're scratching your head thinking, "But Gregg, I want to **talk** to him and get to **know** him on a deeper level."

Yeah, I get it, but let's read my first paragraph again. Men like action.

To that end, if you don't want to take him on the first type of date I suggested, take him on a date doing something he enjoys. If he's a huge basketball fan, offer up going to a game as a date. If he's a hockey fan, go to a hockey game or football or whatever. It doesn't need to be sports either. Maybe he's into old cars or airplanes. Suggest going somewhere where you can look at some old cars or check out airplanes.

What's important here is that you're showing interest in something he likes. Even if you don't know the first thing about basketball, you can get him to believe you do and that you have a similar interest. If you truly do have a similar interest, even better. You might even be able to combine two of your interests. For example, if you're into photography and he loves old cars, you can take your camera along and photo him next to some of his favorites.

Whatever you do, your goal is to let him believe you share an interest—that you're similar in that way. More importantly, you're accomplishing this by *doing things together,* not talking. The last thing most men want to do is sit across from you and have a three-hour feelings talk over appetizers, dinner, and dessert. You say, "Let's go bowling tonight" and he's there with bells on!

Can the two of you have dinner together? Sure, but if you want him to fall in love with you, you're better off to help him know that you're interested in what he's interested in so he will see how well you fit into his life.

When Dining Out

If your date does include dinner somewhere, make it somewhere that won't break the bank. The last thing you want is for a new man in your life to think you're only into him for his money. How do you do this?

You suggest a *quaint little place* for dinner. Translate quaint little place into nice but not expensive. Don't suggest the $50/plate steak joint in the heart of Expensive-ville. Suggest the little hole-in-the-wall Italian place with great lasagna or the cute little burger joint just down from the bowling alley. I know you want to go somewhere fancy but save that date for a special occasion and a time later when he knows for sure you're not just looking for a sugar daddy.

Let Him Be A Guy

Let's face it, nobody is perfect, least of all men. Some men are perfect gentlemen and were raised to hold out the chair for a lady, take her coat, etc. but some men weren't. Regardless of your man's flaws, for heaven's sake don't make a big deal out of them.

Chances are he's trying hard to impress you and he had absolutely no intention of embarrassing himself with gas or clumsiness. Let things go. If you really like this guy, you can subtly work on his manners later. If you make a joke or even kindly dismiss what happened, his feelings for you will immediately decline. Allow him his little screw-ups, after all, he is just human!

What to Wear

I know, I know. You're already stressing over what to wear on a first date and you haven't even met the guy yet. Women amaze me this way, and I grew up with 3 older sisters! Let me clue you in. He won't notice what you're wearing if he's attracted to you. He'll be too busy imagining what you look like without all those clothes on. Stop stressing over clothes. I know I said earlier that he might remember later, but what I'm saying is that wearing the right outfit isn't how you impress him.

By the same token, again, cut him some slack. Men are usually clueless about clothes. Not all of them but many of them. He didn't give 5 minutes of thought to what he pulled out—and he should have. He pulled out the first thing he saw that wasn't: walking to the laundry basket by itself; wrinkled past recognition; stained from last week's pizza after work; or smelling like the soccer field. That probably left him with very few options. Men don't know a thing about 'black belt means black shoes' so don't cut him down to size for it. Men don't always understand why it's wrong to put on a stripe shirt with plaid shorts or something similar. It's clean, it smells good—take what you can get.

Now, what you do want to pay attention to is your hair, makeup, nails and your smile. Remember before I said red or pink lipstick! Men are much more tuned into these details than what you're wearing.

A Bit About Your Drill Sergeant

As one of Boston's top dating coaches, my books rest prominently atop the dating advice genre. In my role as a life coach, I've been known to be unorthodox, in a good way, and I break a few rules. I assist both men and women and help them understand one another.

I won't bore you with my professional bio. Instead, I will share with you the story of how I became a dating and life coach and what makes me qualified to coach you.

The irony of my story is that I come from an extremely dysfunctional family. I witnessed the marriage of my parents crumble before my eyes at an early age. Flying dishes seemed normal in my household. I came out a bit angry and I have 12 years of failed relationships to show for it.

Fortunately, I started encountering positive things in my life. I discovered that couple, that elusive, elderly couple still holding hands in the park at the ripe old age of eighty. They gave me hope. As a problem solver, I could solve anything...except relationships, damn it!

I couldn't figure out why my folks represented the norm rather than the exception to married life. Fifty-five percent of all marriages end in divorce. Why? "What is wrong?"

In 2009, after a long stretch of living the single life, I had an epiphany. I attended a Christmas show at my Dad's church. I am not a religious person, but when I saw the cheerful couples and witnessed the powerful music, I was touched. I needed answers to love and I wanted true love for myself.

I was tired of my shallow single life. I decided to study my failures and interview as many single people and couples as I could. I even watched the movie, Hitch, and it motivated me to help others.

I realized I possessed a natural ability to help others discover love, and knew it was my future. Can you guess where I started? Yep, those happy elderly couples. Sure, I got maced a few times as I approached them with questions, but the knowledge I gained was priceless!

Since then, I have met thousands of people: happy couples, unhappy couples, single people of all types, and everything in between. I quickly learned that confidence played a large role in both attracting and keeping a partner.

My friends encouraged me to launch a dating advice website. I now own the top dating site for women, Who Holds the Cards Now.

Men and women contact me after reading my books. I have become a "Dear Abby" of sorts. Today, after thousands of interviews, I have accomplished my goal. I broke the code and enjoy a great relationship myself. Now I plan to share my findings **with you**!

I have come to realize that even though people believe what I teach, they still suffer a serious problem. They lack the motivation and confidence to execute my tactics. A course change was required. I started concentrating on life coaching in addition to my date coaching. If you can't love yourself, how can you love someone else? It's impossible.

Now, I concentrate on pulling people in and guiding them to understanding themselves. I assist them in creating clarity in their lives, setting goals, and creating the path to attain those goals. I offer inspiration, passion, and spirituality with the constant live like you're dying attitude. People are transformed through my books and daily exercises.

I have written 15 Amazon Best Sellers, four of which reached #1 Best Seller status. Together we can build your confidence, increase your self-esteem, and propel you closer to your goals.

You will discover happiness by completing the work most people will never attempt!

Today, I travel and teach in all the sexy playgrounds: LA, South Beach, and Las Vegas. I can help you in your journey to find love and build confidence so we can transform your life.

I am not merely a best-selling author, my readers are my friends and I communicate with them directly. I humbly ask you to allow me to help you. Join me on my quest for your happiness, your exciting journey to an extraordinary life!

—*Gregg Michaelsen, Confidence Builder*

Get the Word Out to Your Friends

If you believe your friends would draw something valuable from this book, I'd be honored if you'd share your thoughts with them. If you feel particularly strong about the contributions this book made to your success, I'd be eternally grateful if you would post a review on Amazon. My coed motivational books are listed after the women's books on the following pages.

I can be reached at **Gregg@WhoHoldsTheCardsNow.com**.

Please visit my website just for women,
WhoHoldstheCardsNow.com.

Facebook: **WhoHoldsTheCardsNow**

Twitter: **@YouHoldTheCards**

More Dating Advice Books

You can find all my books on the Who Holds the Cards Now Website: www.whoholdsthecardsnow/books

- Who Holds the Cards Now?
- The Social Tigress
- Power Texting Men
- How to Get Your Ex Back Fast
- Love is in the Mouse
- Be Quiet and Date Me
- To Date a Man, You Must Understand a Man
- Committed to Love, Separated by Distance
- Comfortable in Your Own Shoes
- To Date a Man, You Must Understand Yourself
- Middle Aged and Kickin' It
- Manimals
- Pennies in the Jar, How to Keep a Man for Life
- Own Your Tomorrow
- Live Like You're Dying
- The Power to Communicate
- 10 Secrets You Need to Know About Men
- Weed Out the Users, The Couch Potatoes and the Losers
- Night Moves
- He's Gone Now What?
- Riding Solo
- Text Him This, Not That
- When Online Dating Sends You Running for Cover
- Books for Teens
- The Building of a Confident Teen
- Winning the Game of Teen Life